THE WORLD OF DANTE

The World of
DANTE

Six Studies
in Language and
Thought

*Edited by S. Bernard Chandler
and J. A. Molinaro*

PUBLISHED FOR THE DANTE SOCIETY BY
UNIVERSITY OF TORONTO PRESS

To the Memory of Ulrich Leo
1890-1964

Preface

AS PART OF the world-wide celebrations of the seventh centenary of Dante's birth in 1265, the Dante Society of Toronto invited six scholars to address its members during the session 1964–65. Believing that the greatest tribute to Dante lies in the constant acquisition of a deeper knowledge of his work, the Society prescribed no common theme but asked only that each paper should present an original contribution to Dante scholarship, deriving from the speaker's individual thought and research. In consequence, the volume provides a fair indication of at least some of the paths being followed by Dante studies in North America today.

Glauco Cambon presented the first paper, on "Dante and the Drama of Language." Since Italy lacked an established literary language, Dante could not take his medium for granted and was thus compelled to create his own. While Latin represents for him a bridge to other cultures, the language which he develops remains firmly rooted in the vernacular, even in the *Paradiso*. The *Divina Commedia* is a quest for the source of all metaphor. The supreme moment is reached when the poet is overpowered and struck dumb before a vision of the Trinity. This speechlessness has its counterpart in the perversion and negation of language in *Inferno* XXXI, 67: "Raphèl maỳ amèch zabí almí." Dante's mind encompasses the whole range of language from the unintelligible to the ineffable. Between these extremes lies a complex variety of speech out of which grow images of the complex nature of man from Hell to Paradise. Dante, the philosopher of language, should not be overlooked when approaching the *Divina Commedia*.

In the second paper, "The River of Death: *Inferno* II, 108," John Freccero contends that Dante's journey embodies the figure of Exodus, the figure of conversion. We cannot dismiss the Biblical reference in the line "river over which the sea cannot boast" without dismissing the structure of the poem which should be read, in Dante's words, as "the conversion of the soul from the grief and misery of sin to the state of grace." Dante's contemporaries would have understood that the reference to the river, *fiumana*, was to the River Jordan. The *fiumana* "is a death which is a prelude to authentic life," "a descent in humility," before Dante, the pilgrim, can ascend to grace. The only sea which can be compared to the Jordan is the Red Sea, both of which exist in the drama of Exodus. The crossing of the Red Sea represents the figure of Baptism in general, while the River Jordan stands for Baptism in a special sense, as a sacrament bringing grace. Because the River Jordan figures the Baptism of Christ, it is— unlike all other rivers—superior to the sea.

In "The Poet and the Myth of Time," John F. Mahoney continues his previous study of the *Purgatorio* which pointed to the artistic importance in Dante's plan of the historical evidence for the theme of the "second Adam" and the apparent dominance of the Victorine- Augustinian tradition of Incarnational theology in the construction of this *cantica*. He distinguishes between the *stasis* of souls in *Inferno* and *Paradiso* and the *kinesis* of those in *Purgatorio*, who are still changing but whose return to Adam's pristine state is guided, and not erratic, as it was on earth. Through a common *kinesis*, Dante's relationship with the souls in the *Purgatorio* is far closer than with those in the *Inferno* and the *Paradiso*, even though he is still in *tenos*, the state of mortal man awaiting death. Mahoney suggests that Dante followed the "classic" rather than the "Latin" theory of atonement and ends by indicating the importance of time in Dante's conception of Purgatory and so in his plan for the whole of the *Commedia*.

In the fourth essay, "Dante's Three Communities: Mediation and Order," Joseph A. Mazzeo defines the *Divina Commedia* as the "most complete ordering of moral experience." Dante achieves self-definition through Love, "the ordering principle," as he passes from a lower to a higher level of awareness and self-knowledge. Dante can reach his goal only through external mediation, and his journey enables him to define the different states of the will. The damned are in the *Inferno* because they chose the finite and, as a consequence, now find themselves with the "finite eternalized." *Purgatorio* is a com- munity in which the poet encounters exquisite courtesy which gra- dually ripens into charity. Here Dante ceases to be a spectator. In the *Paradiso*, the community of universal truth, the pilgrim's intellectual errors are corrected. The *Paradiso* evokes a life which transcends human experience. Here Dante reduces the discourse of philosophers and theologians to objects of sight. With his newly-acquired powers, Dante, master of the poetry of metamorphosis, sees and becomes one with the love that moves the sun and the other stars. The poem ends in silence and vision.

Gian Roberto Sarolli defines himself as a neopositivist. In his paper, "Dante's Katabasis and Mission," which may be considered a new chapter in his earlier study on "Dante: *Scriba Dei*," he starts from his conviction that the solution of enigmas and difficult lines is essential for the general interpretation of the *Divina Commedia* and of Dante's own life. He investigates the meaning of the words *continga*, *voce*, *vello*, and *cappello* which occur at the beginning of *Paradiso* XXV, taking into account the context of the passage, Dante's usage elsewhere, and the cultural background of the period. His elucidation reinforces his view that the whole structure of the poem is based upon a prophetic urgency. Dante emerges as the exponent of a new theological poetry which is essential for his "katabasis" and mission.

Erich von Richthofen is well known for his extensive publications over the whole field of Romance literature in the Middle Ages, though he has specialized in the epic. His wide background in mediaeval literature is basic to his study on "The Twins of Latona and Other Symmetrical Symbols for Justice." He examines some key concepts and images relating to justice in the *Divina Commedia* and the *Monarchia*, drawn from both classical and later sources, and establishes relationships between them and passages in the preceding epic literature of the mediaeval period.

S. B. C.
J. A. M.

Acknowledgements

IN THE DANTE anniversary year of 1965, the Dante Society of Toronto naturally played a full part, for, while in recent years Canadians of Italian origin have assumed an ever increasing share in the country's development, their contribution to the phenomenal expansion of Toronto in recent years has been fundamental and diversified. At the same time, they have actively participated in the cultural and intellectual life of the city, following the tradition established by James Forneri, the versatile founder of Italian studies at the University of Toronto in 1859.

Mr. Sam Sorbara took the lead in organizing generous support for the Society's ambitious programme of six addresses and their subsequent publication. The aim of the Dante Society—to promote a deeper knowledge of Italian culture among Canadians as one aspect of their common heritage—harmonized with his profound conviction that all men in this country, whether long established or newly arrived, must work together to fashion a new nation, aware of its individual strains yet superior to them, as a distinct entity on which they can look with the pride of achievement. Mr. Sorbara's own career is a striking testimony to his beliefs. Coming from Calabria as a boy, he has combined enthusiasm and constant endeavour to gain eminence in many branches of commerce. He has founded Italo-Canadian organizations and sought always, by understanding and example, to help others follow him in creating for themselves a place in a new society.

Mr. Edward Pasquale, Jr., readily welcomed the project. The elder son of Edward C. Pasquale, who came to Canada from the Abruzzi in 1912, he has developed the firm founded by his father into a major concern manufacturing and importing food products. Prominent in professional and cultural activities, he also finds time to breed some of Canada's finest race horses.

Mr. Michael Simonetta was quick to follow the lead given by Mr.

Sorbara. After coming from Calabria in 1932, he persevered to such an extent in his new country that he was able to establish his own business in Toronto after the Second World War. He has used the position attained to devote himself with equal energy to the field of social service.

Mr. Lanfranco Amato, our other sponsor, is executive vice-president of Olivetti-Underwood in Canada and president of the Italian Chamber of Commerce of Toronto.

To these four benefactors who made our venture possible we offer our deepest gratitude. We should also like to thank Professor Evelyn Rugg and Mr. A. Vicari for their kind assistance, and Professor Giovanni Sinicropi for his advice in the early stages of the project.

Contents

Notes on the Editors
and Authors

S. B. CHANDLER came to the Department of Italian and Hispanic Studies, University of Toronto, in 1957, after holding posts at the Universities of London and Aberdeen. He was President of the Dante Society of Toronto for the Session 1964–65.

JULIUS A. MOLINARO is in the same Department. He founded the Dante Society of Toronto in 1957 and was the Canadian representative on the 1965 Dante Centenary Committee of America.

GLAUCO CAMBON, of Rutgers University, combines an interest in Dante with a wide study of modern literature, especially Italian and American. Apart from numerous articles, he has published *Tematica e sviluppo della poesia americana* (1956); *Recent American Poetry* (1962); *La lotta con Proteo* (1963); *The Inclusive Flame: Studies in Modern Poetry* (1965).

JOHN FRECCERO studied under Charles S. Singleton at Johns Hopkins University and returns there in 1966 from Cornell University, where he has been since 1963. The author of articles on Dante, he has edited *Dante: A Collection of Critical Essays* (1965) which contains essays by prominent critics and scholars of this century.

JOHN F. MAHONEY is Chairman of the English Department at the University of Detroit. He has a background in both English and Classics and a wide interest in mediaeval English, French, and Italian literature. He has published articles on the structure of the *Purgatorio*, on Chaucer, on Andreas Cappellanus, and on Sidney.

JOSEPH A. MAZZEO has been Professor of English and Comparative Literature at Columbia University since 1961. He specializes in Dante and the background of the Middle Ages and in comparative literature of the Renaissance. His *Structure and Thought in the Paradiso* appeared in 1958, *Medieval Cultural Tradition in Dante's Comedy* in 1960, *Renaissance and Seventeenth-Century Studies* in 1964, and *Renaissance and Revolution: The Remaking of European Thought* in 1965.

GIAN ROBERTO SAROLLI, now at the University of California at San Diego, has held University posts in Italy, Argentina, Canada, and the United States. He has published many articles on the mediaeval field, especially a major study in three parts on "Dante: *Scriba Dei*," in *Convivium*, VI (1963). He is also working on the letters of Machiavelli.

ERICH VON RICHTHOFEN has been in the Department of Italian and Hispanic Studies, University of Toronto, since 1964, and has held posts in Germany and the United States. His numerous publications on mediaeval and modern literature deal with Spanish, Italian, French, and German authors. Among his books are: *Alfonso Martínez de Toledo und sein "Arcipreste de Talavera"* (1941); *Studien zur romanischen Heldensage des Mittelalters* (1944); *Vier Lais der Marie de France* (ed.) in 1954, 2nd ed. 1960; *Estudios épicos medievales* (1954); *Veltro und Diana: Dantes mittelalterliche und antike Gleichnisse* (1956); and *Commentaire sur "Mon Faust" de Paul Valéry* (1961).

THE WORLD OF DANTE

Dante and the
Drama of Language

GLAUCO CAMBON

AT THE PEAK of his creative effort, Dante acknowledged crucial difficulties of subject matter:

> perch'a risponder la materia è sorda (*Par.* I, 129)[1]

and of language:

> ché non è impresa da pigliare a gabbo
> discriver fondo a tutto l'universo,
> né da lingua che chiami mamma o babbo   (*Inf.* XXXII, 7–9);

> Oh quanto è corto il dire e come fioco
> al mio concetto! e questo, a quel ch'i'vidi,
> è tanto, che non basta a dicer "poco"   (*Par.* XXXIII, 121–3).

To dismiss such an avowed inadequacy of expressive power as merely a rhetorical device is to ignore Dante's lifelong concern with problems of language—a concern which became actual drama and myth, thereby feeding the very work it might have been expected to undermine. Like so many of our representative modern writers all over the West, though for very different reasons, Dante could not take his own language for granted, and a career of ceaseless struggle with the medium was the consequence. Long before Mallarmé or Eliot he knew what it cost to "purify the dialect of the tribe," the more so as this dialect had to be broadened, and to some extent even invented, before it could be purified. If he had only worried about purity, he

---

[1]All textual quotations are from *Le opere di Dante—Testo critico della Società dantesca italiana* (2nd. ed., Firenze, 1960).

would never have developed into the powerful epic writer we know. He was not Petrarch.[2]

For Dante, as for the experimental moderns, there was a language to repossess; but in his case it was a language in the making and not a worn-out one to be reactivated by some stylistic iconoclasm. He had a culture to create, we have a culture to save or to reject (depending on how we feel about our massive heritage). In either case, it seems fair to say that the contemporary agony of European culture can find itself mirrored, symmetrically, in the growth crisis of Dante's world. The attendant apocalyptic mood led him to take the posture of a prophet, a posture familiar to such contemporaries of ours as T. S. Eliot, Thomas Mann, or W. B. Yeats, whose bent for Dantean (and biblical) apocalypse is an avowed fact. This helps to explain why Dante's poetry, after an eclipse during the Enlightenment and a Romantic revival which was partly a misinterpretation,[3] has come to sound as close and relevant to our eschatological time as it seemed remote to earlier literary ages. A concurrent reason for this renewed relevance has to be recognized in the present affinity for Dante's

[2]The contrast between Dante's epic ruggedness and Petrarch's lyrical smoothness, first acknowledged by Petrarch himself, is seldom overlooked by modern literary historians, but I hope I am not insisting on the obvious by pointing out how their difference in stylistic development implies a radically divergent philosophy of language. Dante's growth as a poet beyond the limited dreaminess of *La Vita Nuova* goes hand in hand with his growing vindication of the vernacular's literary worth as opposed to the Latin tradition to which Petrarch formally subscribed, to the point of writing most of his work in Latin (and that included the epic poem *Africa*) while looking with some condescension on his own vernacular lyrics. Petrarch's *Canzoniere* narrowed the boundaries of the Italian language in poetry by leading it to specialization, it was he who was the dominating influence on the whole European Renaissance to which Dante's steep peak remained inaccessible. Dante's effort was in the direction of linguistic experiment, variety, and inclusiveness, and he could absorb the folk poetry and language which Petrarch had to exclude from his formalizing style. It would seem, then, that of the two Dante was for centuries the far less imitable poet, contrary to T. S. Eliot's statement made in a changed context. It would also seem that the epic quality of Dante and the lyrical refinement of Petrarch cannot be dismissed as irrelevancies of genre classification when we try to define both artists in a common context. Furthermore, Dante's bold attitude in matters of language choice stands out as the forward-looking one especially when compared to Petrarch's coyness vis-à-vis the vernacular; one cannot help feeling that Petrarch, in this regard, had a regressive effect on Italian literature after Dante had done so much to advance the new linguistic cause.

[3]For a telling assessment of these vicissitudes of Dante's poetry in the English-speaking world, see William De Sua's *Dante into English* (Chapel Hill: University of North Carolina Press, 1964). For valuable documentation to the same effect in a far broader geographic and historical context, see Werner Friederich, *Dante's Fame Abroad, 1350–1850* (Roma: Edizioni di Storia e Letteratura, 1950).

conscious craftsmanship and theoretical awareness of linguistic problems. Besides, as Giulio Marzot has so painstakingly shown,[4] the
apocalyptic temper has its repercussions on his style; and the same is
true of his latter-day brethren.

In talking of Dante's attitude to language, whether in the theoretical
or in the creative sphere, I do not forget that in one sense his predicament (the inability to take his medium for granted) is common to
all authentic writers at whatever cultural juncture they happen to
operate, since every poet will have to transform the given language
of his time and place into a personal style. This unavoidable disparity
between the given and the created language is what has prompted
Luigi Malagoli to discuss "language and poetry in the Divine
Comedy,"[5] and Theophil Spoerri to apply De Saussure's binomial
concept of langue et parole in one of the liveliest among recent interpretations of Dante.[6] But the dynamic ratio of personal style to linguistic convention and heritage is by no means the same in every case,
and it will rise to high tension for someone like Dante, who, lacking
an established literary language (outside of his poetically uncongenial
mediaeval Latin) for his most ambitious purpose, had to constitute
one by founding the tradition of epic poetry in the Italian vernacular.

How dramatic this gesture was in itself, even apart from the
dramatic strength of the resultant accomplishment, can be best judged
by the development of Dante's own thoughts on the history, nature,
and range of the lingua volgare. Partly, they come to a head in the
polemical Trattato I of the Convivio, where he passes from scholastic
diplomacy to fiery invective and prophetic metaphors to vindicate
the worth of his beloved Italian vernacular against learned prejudice
and princely snobbery or political neglect. The claim he makes here

[4]Giulio Marzot, Il linguaggio biblico nella Divina Commedia (Pisa: Nistri-Lischi,
1956). The value of this study lies in its having treated the impact of biblical
language on Dante as an inner affinity and not an external influence. Apart from
this, its introductory chapter has some relevance to my theme because it emphasizes
the Commedia's stylistic pluralism.

[5]Luigi Malagoli, Linguaggio e poesia nella Divina Commedia (Genova: Briano,
1949); Saggio sulla Divina Commedia (Firenze: La Nuova Italia, 1962). Malagoli
is sensitive to the range, variety, and tensions of Dante's style.

[6]Theophil Spoerri, Dante und die europäische Literatur—Das Bild des Menschen
in der Struktur der Sprache (Stuttgart: W. Kohlkammer Verlag, 1963). A memorable
interpretation along Existentialist lines; the emphasis it places on language can be
sampled from the statement that Dante's poetical word is "Geschichtsbildend und
Gemeinschaftsstiftend."

for the *lingua volgare* is limited to its use as a commentary on poems written in the same tongue. Although in the scholastic part of his argument he makes it sound as if this were a way of putting the upstart vernacular in its place since it would be beneath the dignity of changeless Latin to stoop to such a low scholarly service, the tone is unmistakable. Eloquence supersedes syllogistic diplomacy when it comes to asserting the personal relevance of *lingua volgare* to the author, whose very existence is shown to derive from the operation of that living everyday speech which had been instrumental in bringing together his father and mother, and striking similes begin to sparkle through the texture of rationalizing rhetoric: fire, hammer, and knife to exemplify the generative power, house on fire to allegorize the force of his love for the native language (*Conv.* I, xii, xiii).

By the end of the chapter, when Dante envisages himself as the dispenser of the new (linguistic-literary) bread of life to coming generations, and actually compounds this evangelic metaphor with that of the new sun (the Italian vernacular) which is going to efface the old one (Latin), we see that eloquence in turn is on the verge of transcending itself into poetry.[7] Thus a doctrinal commentary instigated by earlier poetry becomes itself the matrix of further poetry when it focuses on the problem of language—a theme of the utmost aesthetic and existential importance for our roving exile. Nor can we miss, in the underlying movement of imagery, a religious hypostasis: Dante first recognizes his sonship to the vernacular, then takes it in charge as a sacramental food, and ministers to it as a priest would to a godhead revealing its own power through the sun. The parallel to the Eucharist ritual is oddly reinforced by a totemic meal analogy; Dante has invested all his values in the native language, as poet, citizen, and thinker, and it in turn grows into much more than a vehicle of thought; it becomes the symbolic epitome of his ideal community, and as such, a living force to be linked with procreation, food, and light. In Catholic terms, we could say that this beloved medium is in fact, to Dante, the element of a sacrament, and even, to some extent, the divine presence inherent therein. The living language, as contrasted to the fixed and dead one, is the aptest medium for a

[7]For an evaluation of the metaphoric function in *Convivio*, see Benvenuto Terracini, "La forma interna del Convivio," in *Pagine e appunti di linguistica storica* (Firenze: Sansoni, 1956); and also my own essay, "Dante's Convivio and the Dialectic of Value," in *Papers of the Michigan Academy*, XLVI (1961), 563–570.

communion that is both ritual and everyday intercourse. Notice also that when he metaphorically officiates as a priest of language, he is offering as food for the hungry congregation a metaphoric equivalent of his own body: his own poetry in the *lingua volgare*:

Così rivolgendo li occhi a dietro, e raccogliendo le ragioni prenotate, puotesi vedere questo pane, col quale si deono mangiare le infrascritte canzoni, essere sufficientemente purgato da le macule, e da l'essere di biado; per che tempo è d'intendere a ministrare le vivande. Questo sarà quello pane orzato del quale si satolleranno migliaia, e a me ne soperchieranno le sporte piene. . . . (*Conv.* I, xiii, 11–12)

Therefore, to recapitulate, he is the son of language, language being identified with his parents. Then he identifies with it to the point where he is almost a sacrificial victim, and finally he becomes its priestly keeper, with fatherly connotations vis-à-vis the future communicants. From sonhood to fatherhood is a normal reversal of role in the course of a life, but it is exceptional where a whole culture is concerned. Only people like Dante become the fathers of their own language after having been its offspring.

In the *Convivio*, this reversal is more hinted at than actually formulated, but it counterpoints the dramatic reversal of valuation concerning the respective merits of Latin and of the Italian *volgare*; the former is initially given primacy and described as the absolute lord looking down from the turrets of abstraction on the busy servant, the vernacular, then a crescendo of eloquence actually shifts the whole argument to the latter's side, and carries the day for it, at the ecstatic climax. Nothing in the remaining three chapters of the *Convivio*, despite their doctrinal interest, equals this heightening process, in the course of which Dante's prose ranges through much of the modal gamut his masterpiece will rehearse in the subtler modulations of ripe verse. The chapter begins and ends on a personal note, and in between it touches a variety of keys, from the elaborately discursive to the rhetorical and lyrical, with typical outbursts of political invective subsiding into gentler rapture. Such vehemence of anger and prayer we shall find again in the *Commedia*, and it already stamps this manifesto with the essential form of Dante's spiritual dynamism: a perilous oscillation between the extremes of fury and love which recurrently strains the balance of the wronged man's mind. Remember the swoons of Hell and of Heaven, and how the poet clings to the discipline

of strict form as a saving device to protect himself from the centrifugal
pulls of savage passion. Here in the first chapter of the *Convivio* a
kindred urgency makes the poet's voice overheard throughout, and its
vehemence is sparked by the thought of language. For language was
the exile's special trust and salvation. It was indeed his ark of the
covenant in the ordeal of pilgrimage.

At this point it would seem that my initial argument has reversed
itself. I began by speaking of a self-confessed inadequacy in Dante's
language at certain climactic points, and I insisted that, since he could
not take his language for granted, his poetical career became a lifelong struggle with the medium. The *Convivio* instead, in my interpretation, invests language with a sacramental aura and almost deifies
it. If there can be talk of inadequacy here, it could only refer to the
poet himself vis-à-vis his medium, and not to the medium as such,
which he sees as all but holy. Moreover, if the vernacular, raised by
him to epic dignity, was his true shelter in the homeless life he had
to lead after the overthrow of his party in Florence, one would assume
on Dante's part a trustingly restful, not a struggling, attitude to it.
In the *Convivio* he adduces proximity as his first and chief reason for
choosing the humble vernacular over the official language of scholarship; and warm intimacy is indeed the quality of his relationship to
it in these lively pages. What are we to make of this?

The truth is that Dante's attitude to language was very complex,
for it involved emotional, technical, and philosophical factors in
constant interaction, and this (along with the progress of personal
experience) also made for change. We can follow this change from
book to book as he each time rethinks the problems of language which
found a formulation first in chapter xxv of the *Vita Nuova*, then,
several years after, in the memorable opening chapter of the *Convivio*,
then (after a short interval) in the *De Vulgari Eloquentia*, and finally,
as theory which is resolved or infused in the action of poetry, throughout the crowning poem. Whether the change is a process of evolu-
tionary continuity from beginning to end, as an authority like Luigi
Nardi believes,[8] or a more dialectical one, is a secondary question
which a close reading of the texts in due order may help to decide.
But the dramatic complexity of Dante's attitude to language cannot

---

[8]Luigi Nardi, *Dante e la cultura medievale* (Bari: Laterza, 1949), chap. vi ("Il
linguaggio"), 217–247.

be denied. In the *Convivio* itself, for instance, after the mystical accolade he gives to the vernacular in Trattato I, he complains in Trattato III (iii, 14–15; iv, 1–4) about his own language's inadequacy to the ineffable theme of the *Donna gentile*—a statement which clearly anticipates the lines I quoted above from *Paradiso* XXXIII.

We could explain this complexity by keeping in mind what language meant to Dante as a man of his city and nation, as a member of Christendom at large, and as the artist he was. As an artist, he felt both the potential and the limits of his native medium; as a Florentine, he cherished in it a personal heritage, the tradition handed down to him by the ancestors who had made him what he was; as an Italian, he saw it as a pledge of national unity, a fledgling language which had to compete with the Latin so many poets and thinkers and saints had canonized; however, as a Christian, he could not help recognizing in Latin the necessary bridge to other thinking men who spoke different vernaculars, and he realized the limitations of any language. Through the vital medium of language he could retain his roots in several communities, from one of which, the closest to him, he had been violently uprooted, while the amplest of them, the community of scholars and Christians which could not disavow him, existed more as an ideal than as a palpable actuality. Thus he was certainly at home in his native speech, and felt it as a living thing of intimate concern, something to worship and chide in turn, while at the same time endeavoring to extend its powers into those broader, deeper, and higher areas of experience which had not been claimed for it by his predecessors. His relation to it was intimate, but could hardly be restful or simple, and hardly unchangeable despite his constant fidelity to the language which had nurtured him from the cradle and which he in turn adopted for the highest enterprise a poet could dream of.

There is a demonic impatience in every major artist who is reshaping his medium, and lovers' quarrels will be inevitable. The demonic urge shows in the fiery metaphors I mentioned earlier from the end of the first chapter of the *Convivio*: when he says that his love for the native language is as obvious as fire would be in a burning house, he is expressing the complex nature of his relation to it, implying that the vernacular is his inalienable shelter, but that he dwells there not in a peaceful, but in a consumingly restless way. He had to educate what had culturally begotten him; but he never forgot the source, as the persistence of homespun vocabulary and imagery, even in the rarefied spheres of the *Paradiso*, clearly proves.

And then we must consider Dante's awareness of the historical nature of language. As Luigi Nardi points out,[9] this linguistic historicism reaches its fullest form in *Paradiso* XXVI, where Adam says to Dante that not Hebrew (as Dante had earlier stated in *De Vulgari Eloquentia*) but a lost speech was the original language of the human race. Thus our language-conscious poet takes the final step to show that not even the sacred language of the Bible could remain totally exempt from historical vicissitudes. Hebrew was still the revered language of the patriarchs, but it could no longer claim the distinction of having been the first language, the prelapsarian speech, the *Ursprache* of mankind:

> La lingua ch'io parlai fu tutta spenta
> innanzi che all'ovra inconsummabile
> fosse la gente di Nembròt attenta;   (*Par.* XXVI, 124–126)

> Pria ch'io scendessi a l'infernale ambascia,
> *I* s'appellava in terra il sommo bene
> onde vien la letizia che mi fascia;

> e *El* si chiamò poi; e ciò convene,
> ché l'uso de' mortali è come fronda
> in ramo, che sen va e altra vene.   (*Ibid.*, 133–138)

Along with the philosophical implications, one should not miss here the poetical effect. The philosophy points to humanism:

> Opera naturale è ch'uom favella;
> ma così o così, natura lascia
> poi fare a voi, secondo che v'abbella.   (*Ibid.*, 130–132)

and this is not the only passage where the theologically minded Dante can be shown to harbour in himself a budding Humanist, despite Rudolf Palgen's massive effort to deny it by reducing him to his mediaeval sources.[10] The poetry feeds on the repeated vegetal imagery

[9]*Ibid.*, 244–247.

[10]Rudolf Palgen, *Werden und Wesen der Komödie Dantes* (Graz: Styria Verlag, 1955). Palgen seems more preoccupied with refuting any possible relevance of Dante's vision to a humanism in gestation than with doing justice to the actual poetry and thought of the epic singer. His array of mediaeval sources is impressive, and he certainly brings out the extent to which Dante relied on a specifically mediaeval folkloristic tradition that had obliterated or seriously distorted its classical

that comes to a head in this canto with an intimation of Eden-like happiness, and the distance between the prehistoric state Adam remembers and the late station in history from which Dante is enabled to address him is qualitatively intensified by the idea of a lost Edenic speech. It is a matter of epic perspective enhanced by thoughts of language, and by the direct action of language itself, if we pay due attention to the capital sampling of both the Edenic and the Hebrew word for God in a vernacular context. But perspective is a dominant device in Paradise, the metahistorical realm which affords a bird's-eye-view of history and of the "aiuola che ci fa tanto feroci"; in this passage linguistic distance compounds with the chronological distance from the beginning of history itself and with the dizzily exhilarating spatial distance from history's earthly scene to achieve an effect of felt transcendence. That effect can only be transcended in turn by the eventual threshold experience in which all perspective is annihilated, the

> . . . punto che mi vinse,
> parendo inchiuso da quel ch'egli inchiude.   (*Par.* XXX, 11–13)

Thus language in action creates perspective, aesthetic space, in one of the culminating episodes of the *Commedia*, at the point where Dante meets, in Adam, the archetypal earthly father and the father of all language, before the glimpsed visage of the Heavenly Father supersedes all the long progression of earthly ones, from Virgil to Brunetto and Cacciaguida, and makes language renege. For the *Divina Commedia* certainly is, in one central aspect, a long quest for father and mother, and for the source of all fatherhood and motherhood to which all parental images lead. No wonder that, at the last climax of vision, the tried master of language should regressively feel like a babbling baby, since language fails him in the end when confronting in the Creator the supreme fount of love, maternal no less than paternal:

> Omai sarà più corta mia favella,
> pur a quel ch'io ricordo, che d'un fante
> che bagni ancor la lingua a la mammella   (*Par.* XXXIII, 106–108)

In the architectural economy of the whole, the final vision of the Triune God offsets the perverted trinity that Lucifer had embodied at

---

sources. But he makes it a matter of servile dependence and literal transposition, thereby disregarding those aspects in which Dante reshaped his sources for his own purposes.

the end of the *Inferno*, and, correspondingly, language here, confronted by the rapture of ecstasy, reaches its own upper threshold in avowed powerlessness, just as its nether threshold was avowedly touched in the horror of Hell (*Inf*. XXVIII, 1–6; *ibid.*, XXXII, *cit.*). Such dynamic symmetry between the two extreme limits of imaginable experience—infernal harshness and paradisiac speechlessness—also finds a counterpart in the structural relation between Adam's quoting of the aboriginal holy word in the lost Edenic language, and Nimrod's unintelligible outburst in *Inferno* (XXXI, 67): "Raphèl may̆ amèch zabì almì." Just as three-headed Satan is a parody of the Holy Trinity, this babelic utterance is a parody of the primal language Adam and Eve spoke, and the fact that it sounds vaguely like Hebrew sharpens its effect of weird distortion. As readers, we shall be asked to remember Nimrod's cultural disruptiveness when Adam talks- to Dante in a communicable language to mention the incorrupt language of the world's dawn:

> La lingua ch'io parlai fu tutta spentá
> innanzi che all'ovra inconsummabile
> fosse la gente di Nembròt attenta. (*Par*. XXVI, 124–126)

Whatever the various scholarly attempts at deciphering Nimrod's gibberish may have proved, I here take my stand with the poet himself, who has Virgil tell us:

> ". . . questi è Nembròt, per lo cui mal coto
> pur un linguaggio nel mondo non s'usa.
>
> Lasciamlo stare e non parliamo a voto;
> ché così è a lui ciascun linguaggio
> come 'l suo ad altrui, ch'a nullo è noto." (*Inf*. XXXI, 77–81)

I am in no position to demonstrate that there is no occult meaning embedded in the belaboured infernal line, but I would not put it past Dante's wit to have aimed at teasing his commentators by coining something which sounds as if it might have a meaning and yet has no traceable one; for this would suit very well the dramatic purpose of the specific context. Nimrod's lost language is unintelligible to Virgil and Dante, and therefore to us as well, who are supposed to share imaginatively the poet's shock at being threatened by gibberish

which apes language but is actually a non-language. Incom-
cability is here enacted by language as the utterly fallen, inde-
demoniac condition. It supplies a linguistic equivalent of the dull
opacity into which matter gathers around the frozen bottom of Hell,
at the physical and metaphysical centre of sin, and thus it fits the
monstrous mass of the noisy Giant who stands out as the most heinous
monster of the chained company towering all around the lower edge
of Circle VIII because, by building the Tower of Babel, he brought
about the confusion of tongues.

Perversion of language, and disruption of mankind's linguistic
unity, is in Dante's eyes one of the worst offenses against the spiritual
order, and he therefore makes biblical Nimrod a lesser Lucifer who,
by his hybris, dragged busily aspiring humanity into another Fall;
Nimrod is appropriately punished by confinement in a realm of
enormity and meaninglessness. Once again I find myself compelled to
stress, against Palgen's overemphasis on Dante's naïve indebtedness
to mediaeval sources, Dante's potentially humanistic attitude where
civilization is at stake. Here, in *Inferno* XXXI, Dante sets up a
mythical hyperbole of what Roman classics would have called
"hominem barbarum atque immanem" as an infernal foil to what
civilization means: the city as a place of active order, the endowment
of speech as the norm of significant intercourse. One will easily see
that throughout Hell this implicit image of the city counterpoints
the infernal distortion of it, that Hell is indeed the anti-City just as
Paradise is "quella Roma onde Cristo è romano," the transfigured
city.

City, garden, and court, Dante's Heaven is the place of perfect
mutuality in a hierarchy of interrelation, which language repeatedly
manifests in choral hymns; Dante's Hell is the negative of that unison,
the place of discordant uproar, of frozen passion and self-contained
individualism, as Irma Brandeis has shown,[11] and Nimrod's linguistic
unrelatedness precipitates all that into an apt image. Babel is the
negation of Eden and the caricature of Rome-Jerusalem, but since
the very texture of imagery makes Dante's Paradise a synthesis of Holy
City and Celestial Garden, Hell is essentially babelic, a combination
of anti-Garden (the dark wood, the Wood of Suicides) and anti-City

[11]Irma Brandeis, *The Ladder of Vision* (Garden City, N.Y.: Doubleday, 1960).

(the City of Dis), and our transcendental pilgrim's first impression
of it is fittingly babelic:

> Diverse lingue, orribili favelle,
>   parole di dolore, accenti d'ira,
>   voci alte e fioche, e suon di man con elle
>
> facevano un tumulto, il qual s'aggira
>   sempre in quell'aura sanza tempo tinta   (*Inf.* III, 25–29)

"Confusion of tongues" (as John Ciardi has chosen to translate the
beginning of this passage)[12] signals to Dante's receptive ear the phonic
essence of the infernal condition at the very moment of entering Hell,
and the rest of the *Inferno* will verify this aural prologue. Dante's
imagination was keenly auditory no less than visual, and T. S. Eliot,
who has given special emphasis to this latter aspect,[13] would have
come even closer to descrying the roots of his own elective affinity
for the well-travelled Florentine's poetry if he had recognized the
part that linguistic awareness plays in it, and for that matter in the
initially discontinuous progression of theoretical prose which started
as early as the *Vita Nuova* to be finally reabsorbed in the living tissue
of the major poem. Against Eliot's Crocean contention that Dante's
mind was especially suited to the creation of great poetry because it
could not be "violated by ideas" I would bring the evidence of the
Convivio, where the drama of ideas is unleashed by the author's extant
poetry and clearly points to his future poetry, which it helps to kindle.
Between Dante the thinker and Dante the poet there was a lifelong
cycle of action and reaction which came to its consummation in the
Commedia, for however much of a "naïve poet" he may have been
(in Karl Vossler's Schillerian sense of the word),[14] he contained in
himself a restless critic and philosopher who kept challenging the

---

[12]*Dante, The Inferno*, a new translation by John Ciardi (Mentor Books, 1954),
42. Though Ciardi's version sometimes distorts or cheapens Dante's text (as in
the Ulysses episode), it often brings out relevant implications, as here.

[13]T. S. Eliot, *Dante* (London: Faber & Faber, 1929); *Selected Essays* (New York:
Harcourt, Brace and Co., 1950).

[14]Karl Vossler, *La Divina Commedia studiata nella sua genesi e interpretata*, tr.
Iacini (Bari: Laterza, 1909; English transl. by Lawton, *Medieval Culture—An
Introduction to Dante and his Times*, London and New York, 1929). The introductory chapter compares Dante and Goethe as outstanding examples of the *Naïver
Dichter*, the artist of the native, spontaneous, and whole, as opposed to the *Senti-
mentalischer Dichter*, who is intellectually split by the effort to regain the lost source
of native vision.

poet to self-transcendence; and nowhere does this come out so markedly as in his writings on language, which throughout his career brought out in him the philosophical theorist along with the craftsman and the mythmaker.

These writings culminate in *De Vulgari Eloquentia*; and their very sequence is a drama.[15] Chapter XXV of the *Vita Nuova* deals with the limits of the historically recent vernacular and with the responsibilities of the poet, who pledges himself to raise it from its literary infancy by making it carry all the suitable burden of meaning within what still seems its only legitimate province—that of the short love lyric. He is conscious of having a young language to grow with, and he vows to supersede his "gross" predecessors in the art of verse by looking up to the normative example of the Latin classics, whose figures of speech were never devoid of significance. Many years later, the *Convivio*, as we saw, sanctioned the use of the vernacular in learned commentary on vernacular poetry and widened the gap between Latin and the *volgare* to the extent of incommensurability, only to shift the balance in favour of the latter; and the three chapters of textual explication which follow the linguistic manifesto of Trattato I to illustrate its principles in concrete detail, go far beyond the initial assumptions of the *Vita Nuova* because they come to terms with his actual poetic practice since the composition of that treatise. Now we see that poetry in the vernacular is by no means limited to the subject of courtly love, and in fact it may carry the allegorical weight of ethics, cosmology, and theology, or grapple with the issues of politics in a straightforward way.

Then, with the praise of Lady Philosophy at the end of chapter IV, the *Convivio* stops short of the projected length, since only three *canzoni* have been explicated instead of the intended fourteen; the author is now entirely absorbed by the task of inditing a "booklet"

[15]My idea of that chronological sequence follows Luigi Nardi's position rather than Bruno Migliorini's thesis as set forth in *Questioni e correnti di storia letteraria* (Milano: Marzorati, 1949, chap. I: "La questione della lingua," 1–75), for I see the *De Vulg. El.* as subsequent to the *Conv.* and not simultaneous. This much I gather from internal evidence in *Conv.* I, v, 10: "Di questo si parlerà altrove più compiutamente in uno libello ch'io intendo di fare, Dio concedente, di Volgare Eloquenza." And if we keep in mind the dialectical movement of Dante's linguistic thought from *Conv.* I to *De Vulg. El.*, we cannot escape the inference that the Latin treatise came after *Conv.* I, even if its composition may have overlapped with that of the remaining chapters or Trattati.

on *Volgare Eloquenza* which he had announced in the *Convivio* I,
v, 10. But his creative urgency has risen to breathtaking pitch and
even the pioneering *De Vulgari Eloquentia*, a work important enough
in its own right to be considered the first European treatise on historical linguistics, will stop short of completion to make room for the
all-encompassing poetical endeavour to which it has served as doctrinal
prelude. It will be his special grace, and our good luck, that he just
manages to carry out this ultimate project to which the previous two
have been sacrificed.

A pentecostal frenzy animates these years around 1305–7 which
see enterprise supersede enterprise in a crescendo of work; and we
cannot help noticing that it is a climactic meditation on language, the
central theme of Dante the thinker, that spurs Dante the poet to
his definitive undertaking. How far behind the *De Vulgari Eloquentia*
has left the chronologically contiguous and partly overlapping *Convivio*, as regards the philosophy of language, can be appreciated when
one considers that the vernacular is now openly called "nobler," not
just emotionally closer, than Latin; that it qualifies for the lofty or
"tragic" style in verse; and that its proven mutability no longer marks
it as inferior to the unchangeable *gramatica*, but simply places it in
the historical predicament of life along with the other vernaculars,
whereas Latin is now seen as a constructed language of litterateurs.

The vernacular's literary relationship to Latin, which in the *Vita
Nuova* was conceived as submissive apprenticeship without prospects
of full emancipation, and in the *Convivio* as perfunctory obeisance
in actual estrangement, is now dialectically refocused on the principle
of open autonomy. Open, and not closed, because after the *Convivio*'s
declaration of limited independence, now supplemented by a total one,
the vernacular can afford to compete with the vehicle of Latin
classics on its own ground, without uneasy admissions of semantic or
aesthetic inferiority. Competition implies the acknowledgment of a
model to emulate; the model is recognized in the formal achievement
of the Latin writers, the "regular" writers (*poet[a]e regulati*) who
committed their excellence to an artificial medium (the *gramatica*)
especially devised to universalize their thoughts in geographic space
and stabilize them in historic time. Servile imitation is out of the
question; the vernacular is the spontaneous, the concrete language of
all ("vulgarem locutionem asserimus, quam sine omni regula, nutricem

imitantes, accipimus"), while Latin is an abstract "locutio secundaria" and "potius artificialis" of the learned few (*De Vulg. El.* I, 1, *passim*). And yet, when it comes to literary usage, the spontaneous tongue can look to the "grammatical" one for formal guidance, spontaneity and convention being the two poles of linguistic reality for Latin, Greek, and (if we follow Dante's obvious trend of thought) highly literate peoples anywhere. Dante firmly places himself at the pole of spontaneity, and he establishes the ideal as well as the historical priority of the spontaneous language, that is, vernacular speech, over the institutionalized one (*De Vulg. El.* I, viii–ix).

This revolutionary conception, not to be superseded in its essence (as Spoerri has seen), explains why Dante will feed so much earthy idiom into the fabric of his rigorous epic structure, where on the other hand the guiding function that a formalized literary language like Latin can perform for the developing vernacular finds its dramatic embodiment in one aspect of the relation between Virgil and his ward. Even the fact that Virgil eventually proclaims his disciple's emancipation and leaves him to his own devices on top of Mount Purgatory seems to reflect something of the dynamic relation of vernacular to Latin poetry as ultimately outlined in the *De Vulgari Eloquentia*. It must be said that in his treatises Dante apparently confuses the Latin of the classical poets he knew with the Latin of the Schoolmen, which he himself adapted to his purpose in the *De Vulgari Eloquentia* as well as in the *De Monarchia* and in the *Epistole*; the former would have qualified for the guiding function he ascribes to *poet[a]e regulati* in the *De Vulgari Eloquentia*, while the latter is more probably what prompted him to assign priority to the vernacular.

But if he shows critical naïveté in this regard, he does exhibit a remarkable problematical awareness of what the vernacular as such is, and he thus accomplishes another qualitative leap beyond the level of understanding already reached in the *Convivio*, where there was no question of defining scope and variations of the *lingua volgare*, but merely of identifying it emotionally to justify its use in a broad philosophical inquiry. The *Convivio* simply assumed the vernacular's identity along with its existence; the *De Vulgari Eloquentia* recognizes its factual existence but inquisitively probes its many-faceted identity in a specifically linguistic perspective which has become emphatically national and European. By narrowing his theme to the problem of the nature, history, and uses of the vernacular tongue, Dante has discovered its complexity, which he materializes in the bestiary-like image of the nationwide "wood" (*silva*) to be ranged in hunting for the elusive "odorous panther" of *volgare illustre* (*De Vulg. El.* I, xi, xiv, xv, xvi).

For he realizes that the vernacular is not one, but many: three main families of vernaculars in Europe, three closely related national vernaculars within the Latin area of the continent, and fourteen regional dialects in the Italian peninsula, with endless municipal variations:

Quapropter, si primas et secundarias et subsecundarias vulgaris Ytalie variationes calculare velimus, et in hoc minimo mundi angulo, non solum ad millenam loquele variationem venire contigerit, sed etiam ad magis ultra. (*De Vulg. El.* I, x, 9)

Such multiplicity becomes intractable to the writer in search of a nationally acceptable medium (*volgare illustre*), and Dante concludes that the latter can be found nowhere and everywhere, namely, that it inheres to some degree in every regional and municipal dialect of Italy as an essence, to be limited to no particular part of the peninsula. Here the linguistic problem becomes the stylistic one, and the standards of elegance and euphony Dante mercilessly applies to the sampled dialects (including his native one) show he has come to take the role of author of his own language; for the *volgare illustre* clearly has to be invented.

Dante's search for his language throughout Italy parallels here what the *Commedia* will dramatize as his search for a haven. Home was nowhere and everywhere for our exile; he was afloat in the wide world:

Nos autem, cui mundus est patria velut piscibus equor, quanquam Sarnum biberimus ante dentes et Florentiam adeo diligamus ut quia dileximus exilium patiamur iniuste . . . (*De Vulg. El.* I, vi, 3)

The epic space Dante is going to range in his poem already makes itself felt in the linguistic space he covers here in the Latin treatise, where problematical awareness and empirical perception intertwine with a mythical urge the *Commedia* is destined to turn to full account. Thus the myth of the Tower of Babel, which we found to be focal to the whole *Inferno* and not only to the one canto of the Giants, already serves to structure the problem of the multiplication of tongues, that is, their historical differentiation, in chapters vi, vii, and viii of *De Vulgari Eloquentia* I; and Dante's observant eye imagines the details of the original linguistic catastrophe (I, vii, 6–7) with a zest that reminds us of a painting by Brueghel rather than of the absolutely laconic biblical source of this myth.

The man who cared so much for the spiritual and political unity of mankind could not help feeling that the confusion of tongues had been a second Fall for the descendants of Adam; hence his implicit emphasis on the role of the poet as a cultural unifier of his people, to counteract the disruptive effects of the babelic fall at least within one ethnic area. The bewildering richness of unstable human languages matched the unruly proliferation of strife-ridden local governments, and Dante tended to envisage it as a form of historical entropy to be redressed by creative action. Man was the "mutabilissimum et instabilissimum animal," who had to make the best of his fallen condition. Of course Dante seems to waver between a degenerative and an emergent conception of linguistic history; in *Paradiso* XXVI, the passage he puts on Adam's lips does not consider the multiplicity of tongues a sign of corruption, and in the *Convivio* and *De Vulgari Eloquentia* the fervour with which he espouses the vernacular as the pledge of future historical life contrasts with the grim philosophy he has outlined in his myth of Babel.

Whether dialectically resolvable or not, these tensions contribute to make Dante's approach to language a dramatic one; witness the telling instance of the *De Vulgari Eloquentia* I, iv, where Dante reshuffles Genesis a bit to paint his grandiose scene of the first man talking to God in answer to God's question as mediated verbally by the compliant cosmic elements. Apparently disregarding the beginning of the Gospel of St. John, Dante here says that the word is exclusively human, not divine; and in the two previous chapters he has made language the human endowment par excellence, between the silence of God and Angels on the one hand, and that of demons and brutes on the other.[16] This protohumanist myth can be in itself

[16]For reasons of artistic expediency, Dante, in the *Commedia*, often makes the devils talk, as in Malebolge, or in the case of Plutus, whose cryptic outburst, "Pape Satàn, aleppe," has busied ambitious commentators as much as Nimrod's has. Thus it cannot be said that in this regard the major poem always confirms the interesting myth of *De Vulg. El.* It remains true that Dante feels the articulate word is the essentially human endowment; and he feels this philosophically as well as poetically.

the key to a deeper understanding of Dante's major poem, which
explores the whole spectrum of language from the infra-red threshold
of demoniac unintelligibility to the ultra-violet threshold of paradisiac
inexpressibleness. In between these extremes, the whole range of
speech unfolds, to create from its own protean resources as many
images of man as Heaven and Hell, and the intermediate realm, can
contain.

For it is language in action that evokes Francesca. She is pure voice,
and she haunts the poet who conjured her from the dark whirlwind
with his "affettuoso grido." She haunts us, a complete presence as
nothing visual can ever be. She is a gesture of language. And Farinata
posits his essential reality, and his tangled bond to the fellow Florentine, by a dramatic act of speech which is recognition of their common
language in the most unlikely of places:

> O Tosco che per la città del foco
> vivo ten vai così parlando onesto,
> piacciati di restare in questo loco.

> La tua loquela ti fa manifesto
> di quella nobil patria natio
> a la qual forse fui troppo molesto. (*Inf.* X, 22–27)

Speech is the bond between the living and the restless dead, and
between the two inimical exiles. Cavalcante, an apt foil to the conten-
tious Ghibelline giant, is entirely portrayed in his anxiety by the ham-
mering, broken questions he addresses to Dante; and a misinterpreted
inflection of his interlocutor's language in the cautious reply—a past
tense in the verb referring to Cavalcante's son—is enough to plunge
the pathetic man into howling despair, which the pitch of the voice
and the panting pauses effectively convey:

> . . . . Come
> dicesti? elli ebbe? non viv'elli ancora?
> non fiere li occhi suoi lo dolce lome? (*Inf.* X, 67–69)

Disembodied Pier delle Vigne exists exclusively in the urgency of his
talk, and in the mimetic mannerism of his style; and he takes shape
in the excruciating effort of spilled blood to become word:

> Come d'un stizzo verde ch'arso sia
> da l'un de' capi, che da l'altro geme
> e cigola per vento che va via;

> sì de la scheggia rotta usciva inseme
> parole e sangue . . .   (*Inf.* XIII, 40–44)

Likewise, Ulysses' struggle with the swathing fire enacts the dramatic birth of language:

> Lo maggior corno de la fiamma antica
> cominciò a crollarsi mormorando
> pur come quella cui vento affatica;
>
> indi la cima qua e là menando,
> come fosse la lingua che parlasse,
> gittò voce di fuori . . .   (*Inf.* XXVI, 85–90)

He is a tongue of flame, his own torment and catharsis; he is like the odyssean poet from Florence who lived by that which consumed him. He is a Pentecost in Hell; we see him only as a stubborn glow, and we touch him in the muscular movements of his recapitulating voice. That other flame, sinuous Guido da Montefeltro, the reverse of Ulysses in so many ways, also takes shape for us as a pure creation of the inflected word, and lives as a kinetically aural image right from the start when his fiery pain strives to become language:

> Come 'l bue cicilian che mugghiò prima
> . . .
> mugghiava con la voce dell'afflitto,
> . . .
> così, per non aver via né forame
> dal principio nel foco, in suo linguaggio
> si convertìan le parole grame.   (*Inf.* XXVII, 7–15)

Especially in this Bolgia of the Evil Counselors where language is the agent of damnation, we find the poet, his guide, and his interlocutors very sensitive to linguistic nuances: thus Virgil intercedes for Dante with Ulysses and Diomede to make them speak, for they are Greek and might be inaccessible to Dante's native speech (*Inf.* XXVI, 70–75); and Guido is impelled to address Dante because he overhears his North Italian cadence (*Inf.* XXVII, 19–21). As elsewhere, Dante the poet is helped by Dante the linguist, and the *De Vulgari Eloquentia* looms once again behind the *Divina Commedia*.

We also remember the poet's own difficulties with his irksome theme, as confessed at the outset of *Inferno* XXVIII and XXXII, when we see him stress Ulysses' and Guido's efforts to overcome their

obstructions to break into articulate speech. Above all, we are then
aware of Dante's dynamic conception of language, a conception which
informs and sustains his creative practice of repeatedly conjuring the
human image as an expressive process. And at the bitter end of Hell,
where ice freezes that image, gushing anger symbolically overcomes
the most infernal obstruction to change it into a cleansing flood:

> Ahi Pisa, vituperio de la genti
> del bel paese là dove 'l sì suona,
> poi che i vicini a te punir son lenti,

> muovasi la Capraia e la Gorgona,
> e faccian siepe ad Arno in su la foce,
> sì ch'elli annieghi in te ogni persona   (*Inf.* XXXIII, 79–84)

There could be no more violent catharsis for the desperate patriot
than this superhuman fury, so ironically counterpointed by the loving
mention of his sweet native speech in that place where wrath is the
only force that can reconvert the ultimate image of death into a
momentary rush of life. After Ugolino, only the mechanical silence
of ogre Lucifer.

That fairytale monster, like the Gulliverian giants of Canto XXXI,
reminds us of *De Vulgari Eloquentia*, where the qualitative difference
of man from demon was posited as the infinite distance between
articulateness and muteness. The same distance is here dramatically
operative. It helps us to feel the impact of the purging which Dante
has undergone in Hell through the ordeal of language, which here
touched its lowest ranges along with its greatest passionate intensity.
Now it can leave behind the *rime aspre*, and the vulgar and the gory
and the excrementitious, as a serpent sheds its skin. In Purgatory the
"dead poetry" will celebrate its "resurrection"; Casella's nostalgic
music will replace the anal trumpets of the devils and Nimrod's
senseless bugle. In Purgatory Arnaut Daniel's Provençal utterance
will supersede the babelic "diverse lingue" with a congenial linguistic
chord, for here multiplicity is no longer anarchy and Babel's caco-
phony yields to polyphony.[17] Arnaut's refining fire, a truer Pentecost

---

[17]The multilingual situation was common to many a mediaeval writer, and we
can find several instances of mediaeval polyglot poetry in the English area, as the
Oxford Book of English Verse shows. German literature was also affected by linguistic pluralism in early mediaeval devotional writing (which included glossaries and
translations of the interlinear kind) and in the early Humanist phase. That was
due to the existence of Church Latin (sometimes supplemented by Greek) as a

than Ulysses', will mark the nearly accomplished second catharsis of our pilgrim shortly before he is ready for the effortless voices of Heaven.

Dante's drama is the drama of his language, which he raised from literary adolescence to fullest maturity. By the time he was writing the *Commedia*, the initially narrow limits of his fledging vernacular had come to coincide with the limits of human language as such. The fact that language never stopped worrying Dante the thinker, the craftsman, and the mythographer, finds appropriate expression in the special distinction the *Divina Commedia* enjoys among the great epics of the West: that of insisting on dramatic utterance, and on the becoming of the word, as its central effect. This is why we should not overlook the philosopher of language in Dante when approaching his conclusive poem. The *Commedia* drew on the *De Vulgari Eloquentia*, even though at several points transcending its conceptions, as poetry must finally transcend even the most germane discursive thought. Thus, for instance, in the *De Vulgari Eloquentia* Dante indicates the limited *canzone* as the only metric pattern for lofty poetry in the vernacular, and in matters of vocabulary he seems to think rather in terms of static purity than of dynamic purging.[18] The

---

ritual and scholarly language, and to the concomitant availability to the budding poet of more than one competing vernacular. In this connection, Italian Sordello's use of Provençal readily comes to mind, and one can also refer to the Franco-Italian contamination which resulted in the *cantores francigenarum* tradition. The testimonial of *De Vulg. El.*, along with Dante's poetic practice, shows that he did not feel Provençal (or even French) to be a really alien language, though he did not like to see it preferred to the Italian vernacular; and while capable himself of writing beautiful verse in *langue d'oc*, he shrank from contamination. Teofilo Folengo's invention of Macaronic Latin would have puzzled him; his own experiment with linguistic coinages (of the possibly contaminating kind) was restricted to the focally babelic utterances of Plutus and Nimrod, as examples of perverted language. Dante's linguistic axis is the Italian vernacular, but he is conscious of functioning in a multilingual context, and his discriminating amity to Provençal and Latin may remind us of the "multi-dialect" approach which led classical Greek writers to stabilize Doric as the language of the tragic chorus, Ionic as the language of tragedy and epic, and Attic as the language of prose. Dante's use of frequent Latin inserts from Church ritual in the *Divina Commedia* certainly adds to the epic's linguistic dimensions, though these dimensions avoid the confusion of hybridism because they function separately within the main framework as perspectival devices. For a provocatively succinct treatment of mediaeval complexities of language and their modern counterparts, one can see Gianfranco Contini's preface to C. E. Gadda's *La cognizione del dolore* (Milano: Einaudi, 1962), and also references in S. Avalle d'Arco, "Lingua, stile e scrittura" in *Questo e Altro*, VIII (Milano, 1964).

[18]My point is that linguistic pluralism was one of the cultural experiences Dante used to dramatic advantage in his poem, and it could become babelic in its infernal

Divina Commedia will burst those bounds. But in one fundamental point the final poem verifies the preliminary speculation: that of making language the specifically human act. Out of whatever tensions and raptures, over and over again the Dantean characters say to us: *Loquor, ergo sum.*

---

aspect, polyphonic instead in its purgatorial or paradisiac one. Structurally, that is a conversion of the unrelated to the harmonized multiplicity; of history as Fall to history as Redemption. I speak of polyphony because I think of the individuality each poetical voice (and each soul) retains in the ascending chorus. And I would like to add that the polyglot trait of mediaeval writing constitutes a generally overlooked precedent for Dante-inspired moderns like Ezra Pound, T. S. Eliot, and James Joyce. In *De Vulg. El.* II, vii, Dante approaches a purist position in matters of word choice for the lofty ("tragic") style in poetry; he eliminates "childish" (*puerilia*), "womanish" (*muliebria*), and "virile, but uncouth" (*virilia . . . silvestria*) vocables, and concentrates on two varieties of "virile-urban" words, the "smooth-combed" (*pexa*) and the "tough" or "rugged" (*irsuta*), which qualify as "grandiose" (*grandiosa*), to the exclusion of the "slippery" and "coarse" ones (*lubrica et reburra*). The "tragic" poets in the vernacular must use only *vocabula nobilissima*; examples of the rejected word types are, among others, *mamma e babbo, placevole, greggia, cetra, femina, corpo.* This flies in the face of stylistic procedure in all of the *Inferno* and noteworthy parts of the other two Canticles, whose lexical range is far broader than the precepts of the *De Vulg. El.* would allow. Once again, we notice a dialectical movement, rather than a smooth progression in his thought and practice; for here the *Commedia* inverts a basic point of the previous book by incorporating in its style the harsh, the horrid, and the disgusting, as a phase of language to be purged within the actual progress of the poem, and not to be left out a priori. Concessions to the requirements of mimetic style are limited, in *De Vulg. El.*, to admitting *vocabula irsuta* (= blunt monosyllables and heavy polysyllables) in the ennobling company of the preferably trisyllabic, melodious *pexa*; likewise, *rime aspre* (*rithimorum asperitas*), harsh rhymes, are to be avoided unless in proper combination with the sweet ones (*rithimi lenes*) or *rime dolci*, for "lenium asperorumque rithimorum mixtura ipsa tragedia nitescit." It is also remarkable that *tragedia* denotes the lofty style in *De Vulg. El.*, while *Commedia* is the title Dante chose for his epic poem, which moves from the "low" to the "lofty."

The River of Death:
Inferno II, 108

JOHN FRECCERO

IN THE TWENTY-FIFTH canto of the *Paradiso*, as Dante is about to be examined on the virtue of Hope, Beatrice introduces him to St. James as the man to whom it was "granted to come from Egypt to Jerusalem, in order to see, before the prescribed limits of his warfare" (XXV, 55–57). With these words, Beatrice glosses Dante's journey in retrospect, according to the figure of Exodus, the Old Testament story that was taken by mediaeval exegetes to be a foreshadowing of the coming of Christ. By describing this particular journey in terms of the master-plan of Christian history, Beatrice reveals the structural principle whereby the personal experience of the pilgrim is to be understood in more general terms as another embodiment of the continually unfolding pattern of God's providence.

This structural principle, which has been studied by Erich Auerbach[1] under its mediaeval name, *figura*, gave to the otherwise linear course of Christian history (of the self or of the world) a recurrent pattern of meaning. The Redemption was thought to have been adumbrated by the flight of the Jews from Egypt long before the Crucifixion, the event by which it was finally made manifest. Furthermore, both the exodus of the Jews and the Redemption were thought to have their final fulfilment, at least in history, with the Second Coming. At the same time, the drama of Exodus might be embodied in

[1]Erich Auerbach, "Figura" in *Scenes from the Drama of European Literature*, trans. R. Manheim (New York, 1959), on which see the remarks of D. Della Terza in his Italian translation of Auerbach's Dante studies (*Studi su Dante*, Milano, 1963), esp. xiii–xv.

the experience of every individual soul, thereby recapitulating the essential outlines of universal history in the justification of each sinner. So Dante's journey, while preserving its uniqueness as the experience of a single man, nevertheless embodies the figure of Exodus, the timeless pattern that is fulfilled in God. In the *Epistola* to Can Grande, Dante suggests that the poem is to be read according to this figure, by which is signified, among other things, "the conversion of the soul from the grief and misery of sin to the state of grace."[2] We may take it as established by Dante's own words and as demonstrated by Charles Singleton,[3] his foremost critic in our day, that the outlines of the poetic journey are essentially those of Exodus, the figure of conversion.

If this is so, then the journey without a guide, the frustrated attempt to climb the mountain in the first canto of the *Inferno*, must be considered an exodus that failed, a temporary escape that was not a definitive departure from "Egypt," but merely a disastrous sortie. From the pilgrim's perspective, the final barrier on the difficult road to the summit seems to be the wolf; the view from Heaven, however, refers to another, equally formidable, barrier. So we must assume from the words of Lucy when she calls upon Beatrice to help the pilgrim who finds himself blocked, *impedito*, on the desert slope:

> "Non odi tu la pièta del suo pianto,
>   non vedi tu la morte che 'l combatte,
>   su la fiumana ove 'l mar non ha vanto?"   (*Inf.* II, 106–108)

We know a great deal about the nature of this "river over which the sea cannot boast" in terms of the moral theology of Dante's time.[4] A

---

[2] *Epistola* X, 7.

[3] "In Exitu Israel de Aegypto," *78th Annual Report of the Dante Society of America* (Boston, 1960).

[4] Charles Singleton, "Su la fiumana ove 'l mar non ha vanto" (*Inf.* II, 108), *Romanic Review*, XXXIX, 4 (December, 1948), 269–277, to which the reader is referred for the relevant bibliography. Since Singleton's essay, Antonino Pagliaro (". . . ove 'l mar non ha vanto. Dante, Inf. II, 108," *Studi in onore di Angelo Monteverdi*, II (Modena, 1959), 543–548) has attempted a reading of the verse, the most valuable part of which is a survey of previous studies on the subject, excluding Singleton's. As for the reading itself, it is vitiated by an almost total incomprehension of figural principles. See the brief review by Francesco Mazzoni in *Studi danteschi*, XXXVIII (1961) 383–384. Singleton identifies the "fiumana" with the wolf and produces a wealth of citations from the Fathers of the Church in order to show that the river is to be identified with the *fluctus concupiscentiae*. There is no contradiction between his thesis and the present one; this study seeks only to apply some of the insights gained from a reading of Singleton's later work

good deal remains to be said, however, about its figural meaning, that is, its place here in the description of an exodus that fails. It is perhaps because we have been exclusively concerned with the pilgrim's point of view in our attempt to explain these puzzling verses that we have not taken sufficient notice of the fact that they are Lucy's words and that they are spoken in Heaven. It is the purpose of this paper to show that when Lucy speaks of the wolf as though it were a *fiumana*, she is glossing the frustrated journey precisely as Beatrice will later gloss its successful counterpart in the *Paradiso*; that is, according to a *figura* which cannot be perceived by the pilgrim on this side of the river.

Because the exegetical language is no longer familiar to us, it is tempting to dismiss any biblical dimension of meaning as being no longer relevant to a modern reading of the text. To do so in this case, however, would be to dismiss the entire structure of the poem. This becomes apparent as soon as we realize that the "view" from Paradise, being that of the ending of the poem, is the view of the poet himself. In a sense, the purpose of the entire journey is to write the poem, to attain the vantage-point of Lucy, and of all the blessed, from which to perceive the *figura* and the coherence in life, and to bear witness to that coherence for other men. As in all spiritual autobiography, the protagonist struggles to stand outside time and from there to find the meaning of his history and to judge it as though it were concluded. The duality of the imagery in the prologue scene, with the pilgrim using the wolf and Lucy the river as descriptions of the same dramatic action, indicates a dialectic fundamental to this poem or to any novel of the self: the perspective of the self that *was*, corrected and reinterpreted by the perspective of author, the self that *is*. Dante's journey, the story of how he came to write the poem, ends where it began,

---

(cited above) to an understanding of the figural dimension of meaning—the view from the ending of the poem. From the pilgrim's perspective, the barrier seems indeed to be the formidable one of concupiscence, as Singleton demonstrates. To buttress his argument even further, we may point out that the *topos* of the *fluctus concupiscentiae* was not confined to Christianity. In Plato's *Timaeus*, it is precisely a *fluctus* of the senses to which the newly incarnate soul is subjected: "These circuits [of the mind], being thus confined in a strong river, neither controlled it nor were controlled, but caused and suffered violent motions" (*Tim.* 43A). Chalcidius (*ad loc.*, ed. Waszink in the series *Plato latinus* (London, 1962), 223) identifies this "river" as *silva*, prime matter. It is precisely to bring these violent motions under control that the soul requires *paideia*.

when the pilgrim who *was* becomes the poet who has been with us from the beginning. The journey and the poem itself are therefore inseparable; the figure of Exodus is not only the subject-matter of the story, but also, in Dante's view, a pre-condition for the existence of it. Since both the journey of the pilgrim and the struggle of the self to capture its own essence in retrospect depend for their existence on a conversion they may therefore be described according to the traditional biblical figure for such an experience—an exodus from Egypt to Jerusalem—and they take place within the prescribed limits of Dante's life.

Once we think of the barrier facing the pilgrim in the first canto as an impediment not only to the completion of the journey but also to the telling of the story, we begin to see the aptness of describing the encounter as a mortal combat. If the journey had ended there, the poem could never have been written. The fact that we have it before us proves that the pilgrim ultimately survived this struggle. On the other hand, there is a sense in which all self-analysis presupposes a death of the self. To grasp the totality of a historical evolution, it is necessary that the evolution be completed and that the observer stand outside it. Only from Jerusalem could the Jews have written their national epic, for then the myriad extraneous details of the journey could be separated from those events which seemed to reveal the providential structure of their exodus.[5] Similarly, the Book of Exodus could be interpreted as having been prophetic only when read from the perspective of the New Testament as a fulfilment of the Old. However, when the evolution is that of the self, the goal of the journey is death, the necessary conclusion, which terminates the perpetual change of the self so that inventory may be taken. Death being what it is, the inventory must usually be left to someone else. A spiritual autobiography then, in order to be authentic, requires nothing less than death and subsequent rebirth.

Because such a death and resurrection is in ordinary terms unthink-

[5]In an interesting comparative study of "hermeneutic" and "structural" modes of interpretation, Paul Ricoeur, "Symbolique et temporalité," in *Ermeneutica e tradizione*, ed. E. Castelli, Archivio di Filosofia (Padova, 1963) 20–21, 29–31, gives as an example of the former the retrospective exegesis of the Jews on their own history. He fails to note, it seems, the "detachment" required for such self-analysis, represented by the Jews as the crossing of Jordan. On the contrary, that detachment is precisely what allows the self to take a "diachronic" view of itself. *Figura* is a necessarily diachronic way of looking at the self and the world.

able we find few novels of the self that strike us as successful. Those which concern themselves solely with history seem to be devoid of any structure or coherence because there is no definitive separation between the past and present self. No number of historic details amassed by an author can add up to the continuity of a single life. On the other hand, when such novels err on the side of plot, they strike us as too neat and contrived. The rationale superimposed upon the "facts" seems to stifle whatever authenticity those facts may have had. Somewhere between these two forms of literary failure there lies the authentic novel of the self, a story told with all of the intimacy and historicity that comes from the organic continuity of the author with his subject, yet at the same time, with the detachment and sense of finality that seems to come only with death. The *Divina Commedia* is the first and perhaps the foremost of such novels of the self. The retrospective structure of a historic evolution is, in terms of literary creation, the retrospective structure of this greatest of spiritual auto-biographies.

The river of death alluded to by Lucy's words is therefore the boundary separating facile autobiography from the true novel of the self. Short of that barrier, preaching about virtue sounds hollow and meaningless; only the man who has survived a death of the self has the right to exhort others to follow him. That view is somewhat like the panorama seen by a drowning man, who is able to look back over the whole course of his life and to see it in its totality precisely because that life is about to be concluded. We know from the existence of the poem that the pilgrim has in fact managed to cross the river, just as we can know about the panoramic vision in the instant before death only because by some accident a few have survived the drowning. Dante's story seems as gratuitous as that of a man who has survived his own death. The death of his former self is almost an episte-mological necessity for the existence of the story, and at the same time this miraculous event is the story itself. The traditional name for this death and rebirth is conversion, a burial of the "Old Man" so that the "New Man" might be born. The destruction of the former self in preparation for the reception of sanctifying grace was known in Pauline terms as the "Baptism unto death," the descent into the tomb before the ascent to Grace, made possible by Christ's own death and resurrection. In figural terms, it takes place in the "river" before

which the pilgrim is standing when he comes to the attention of
Lucy. His failure to overcome the wolf is a failure to "come over" the
fiumana into the Promised Land. Since Lucy is speaking to Beatrice,
a fellow citizen of the heavenly Jerusalem, she refers to the last stage
of his conversion in terms of the last river, known to all of the elect
as Jordan, which must be crossed before the exodus is accomplished.

The narrative of Exodus may be broken down into three parts: first
there is Egypt, from which the children of Israel escape into the
desert by a miraculous crossing of the Red Sea which opens for them
and closes over Pharoah's soldiers. The crossing of the desert is
accomplished next under the guidance of Moses, with the help of
Heaven. Moses does not, however, fulfil his mission; he dies and is
taken by the Lord before Israel arrives at its goal. It remains for
Joshua to take command and to lead his people into Jerusalem. Once
more, an act of God is required before this can occur, for the river
Jordan is flooded and must be parted by another miracle before Israel
can cross. Thus there are three crucial stages along the way: the
Red Sea, the desert, and the River Jordan, and the journey cannot be
said to be complete until the last step has been taken. Unfortunately,
however, the last stage on the way to perfection is the most difficult
to take, for, to return to the language of the doctrine which underlies
the figure, it is the work of sanctifying grace.

Three physical areas in the prologue scene correspond to these
three figural areas in the drama of Exodus.[6] Immediately after leaving
the dark wood, the poet uses a simile which implicitly relates the
wood to the crossing of a sea:

> E come quei che, con lena affannata,
> uscito fuor del pelago a la riva,
> si volge a l'acqua perigliosa e guata,
>
> così l'animo mio, ch'ancor fuggiva,
> si volse a rietro a rimirar lo passo
> che non lasciò già mai persona viva.   (*Inf.* I, 22–27)

---

[6]Singleton (" In Exitu . . .," *cit.*) has discussed these correspondences between the
Purgatorio and the prologue scene at length. In an article published almost simultaneously with Singleton's, and bearing the same title (in *American Benedictine
Review*), Fr. Dunstan Tucker attempted an over-all reading of the *Purgatorio*
according to the figure of Exodus. He did not, however, mention the correspondence
to the prologue scene. For the general typology of Exodus, I am most indebted to
Jean Daniélou, *From Shadows to Reality*, trans. W. Hibberd (London, 1960), esp.
chaps. IV and V.

The word *passo* associates the open sea with a crossing and thus fore-shadows the first stage of the drama of exodus, which awaits the first scenes of the *Purgatorio* to reach its fulfilment. Again, the mountain slope is first called a *piaggia diserta*, and then a *gran diserto*; we therefore have little difficulty associating the desert slope with the second area of our exodus *manqué*. The problem seems to be only to distinguish the third moment of the prologue from the final "crossing" that is presented to us in the figure of Exodus. That final moment, which proves the pilgrim's undoing, is identified by Lucy when she refers to the pilgrim as weeping on the banks of a *fiumana*, a swollen river, unable to cross without the help of Beatrice. Dante's contemporaries would have had no trouble in identifying it by its figural name: the River Jordan flooded before the Israelites.[7]

Within a Christian context, to speak of a "river over which the sea cannot boast" is necessarily to speak of the Jordan. In order to show this we shall have to look carefully at the verse. The early commentators were inclined to take it literally, as a reference to a stream running at the foot of the mountain or else to the River Acheron itself. The dramatic and poetic difficulties entailed by such an identification appear to be insuperable and for this reason many modern commentators have abandoned it, choosing instead to understand the river as purely metaphorical.[8] The difficulty here is that whatever the ontological status of the river, that status is shared by the sea. *La fiumana* and *il mare* seem to have equivalent modes of existence. It therefore seems unsatisfactory to suggest that the river is superior to the sea because the former has a purely spiritual significance. A totally satisfying explanation would have to account for both the river and the sea on the same plane of reality. Even an uncompromisingly "aesthetic" commentator has insisted that the river is to be understood in the same way as we understand the *pelago* or "open sea" of the simile in Canto I, quoted above.[9] There remains the question of why, on any level of reality, this river should be superior to the sea.

In antiquity, there was one river considered to be superior to any

[7]Joshua: 3–5.
[8]Singleton, "Su la fiumana . . . ," pp. 271–2.
[9]A. Momigliano (*ad loc.*): "Vi è ripresa in forma diretta e più impressionante l'immagine del 'pelago' . . ."

sea: *Oceanos*, the father of all waters.[10] Homer describes it in the *Iliad*:

> . . . the deep and powerful Stream
> of Oceanos, the source of all rivers,
> every sea, and all the springs and
> deep wells that there are. (XXI, 196)

In the mythological cosmology of Homeric Greece, the river was thought to be the boundary of all reality. For this reason, the shield of Achilles had for its rim "the mighty Stream of Oceanos" (XVIII, 607). Beyond the boundary formed by the river lay the world of the dead, into which the river carried those who crossed it. Circe sends Odysseus to "the deep-flowing River of Oceanos and the boundaries of the world" (*Odyssey* XI, 21) in order to arrive at the kingdom of Hades. Eventually, the river was personified as a kindly old god and came to represent water itself.[11]

An analogous theme concerning the cosmological waters of the kingdom of the dead seems to have existed among the Jews. The waters of Tehom were the realm of the dead, sometimes appearing above the earth but more often beneath it as the black waters of chaos.[12] In the Book of Enoch, the prophet in his journey reaches the great river and the darkness of the west.[13] It therefore comes as no surprise to cultural historians to find such ideas prevalent among Christians too. Their great river was the Jordan. In the Gnosis, the Jordan was a cosmic river, the frontier between the world of the senses and the spiritual world.[14] In orthodox Christianity, the Jordan was associated with the rivers of Paradise and came to represent all waters, purified by the Baptism of Christ.[15] It was perhaps inevitable that Christian ideas about the "sacramental" and "cosmic" character of the Jordan should come to be associated with the mythology of

[10]On Oceanos, I have consulted the usual handbooks on classical literature. By far the most useful is the article by P. Weizsäcker in Röscher, *Lexikon* III, col. 809–820 (*s.v.*).

[11]Werner Jaeger, *Paideia* I (1934), 207, cited by G. M. A. Hanfmann in *Oxford Classical Dictionary*, *s.v.*

[12]Per Lundberg, *La typologie baptismale dans l'ancienne église* (Uppsala, 1942), 64–72.

[13]Book of Enoch XVII, cited by Lundberg, 69.

[14]Lundberg, 151 ff.

[15]See the chapter entitled "Der Paradiesjordan" in F. Ohrt, *Die ältesten Segen über Christi Taufe und Christi Tod* . . . Det Kgl. Danske Videnskabernes Selskab. XXV, 1 (Copenhagen, 1938), 180 ff.

Oceanos, the source of all waters, the boundary between life and death and hence the entrance to the Other World.[16] By a logical extension of these associations, the name of Oceanos was also evoked within the context of Exodus. The earliest such evocation seems to be in a report by St. Hippolytus on the teaching of the Naassenes:

The Ocean is the birthplace of the Gods and of men: ever flowing backwards and forwards, now upwards, now downwards. When the Ocean flows downwards, then men are born; when it flows upwards, then are the gods born. . . . All that is born below is mortal: all that is born above is immortal, for it is begotten spiritual, of water and the spirit. . . . This is said of the great Jordan, whose current, when it flowed downwards, prevented the children of Israel when they left the land of Egypt from entering, was arrested and made by Jesus-Joshua to flow the other way.[17]

Thereafter, the association between Oceanos and Jordan became a commonplace. The theme of the flux and reflux of the river, inherent in the folklore of the cosmic river, was reinterpreted in terms of the figure of Exodus.

This early mythological association will perhaps help to explain why the River Jordan is often personified by a thoroughly pagan river god throughout the history of baptismal iconography, at least until the Carolingian period and somewhat beyond it.[18] It also helps to explain why it should have been the object of fanciful geographic speculation in the Middle Ages—it was thought by some geographers that the river continued its course underground to reappear later at its own source.[19] Some commentators on Dante's poem, notably

[16]Lundberg has made much of the "Okeanos-Jordan" in Mandaean sects. The problem is crucial, for some (Reitzenstein, among others) have attempted to show that the importance of the Jordan in primitive Christianity reflects a Mandaean and ultimately oriental influence on Christianity. See Daniélou, 272, Lundberg, 155 ff.

[17]Translation from Daniélou, 273, quoted from Hippolytus, Elenchos V, 7; Patrologia Graeca, 16, 313f. Daniélou does not mention the fact that Hippolytus is here fusing a quotation from Odyssey XXIV, 9 with Psalm 82:6–7.

[18]See the discussion of Ferdinand Piper, Mythologie der Christlichen Kunst (Weimar, 1851), II, 489–564 for an exhaustive account of the iconography of the river in Christianity. Throughout the chapter, the personification of the Jordan is discussed, the material being chronologically, rather than thematically, arranged.

[19]Ohrt (177 ff.) reviews the history of cosmographical speculation about the Jordan in his chapter "Der Weltjordan." He notes that already in the Talmud the Jordan was imagined to continue its course from the Dead Sea into the great sea (Bekhoroth 55ª; Strack-Billerbeck 1:101). He continues the history of this speculation in the Arabic cosmographers of the Middle Ages. Of special interest to us is this conclusion: "der Jordan ist Hauptstrom des ganzen irdischen Wassersystems . . . ." (177).

Grandgent, have suggested that the characteristic of not flowing into the sea was enough to qualify a river as "la fiumana ove 'l mar non ha vanto." If this were the case, then the Jordan would qualify as well as the Acheron, Grandgent's identification.[20] The spiritual importance of the Jordan in the Baptismal liturgy led very early to statements about its geographic "transcendence" in terms reminiscent of the descriptions of Oceanos in antiquity. Gregory of Nyssa, for example, speaking of the Jordan, insists upon its cosmic importance:

> For indeed the river of grace flows everywhere. It does not rise in Palestine to disappear in some nearby sea: it spreads over the whole earth and flows into Paradise, flowing in the opposite direction to those four rivers which come from Paradise, and bringing in things far more precious than those which come forth. . . .[21]

In this passage, there can scarcely be any doubt that the mythology of Oceanos is operative. The Jordan qualifies as a Christian Oceanos and is for this reason superior to any other body of water.

Of particular interest to the student of Dante in this admittedly remote conflation of mythological ideas is the association of these rivers, not only with death, but also with the *descensus ad inferos*. We have seen that in Homer the great river was considered a gateway to the Other World. This was also the case with the "Great Jordan" in early Christianity. Per Lundberg has demonstrated that the descent into the river was traditionally seen as a victory over death and the devil and therefore was analogous to Christ's victory in the Harrowing of Hell.[22] The victory took place between Christ's death and Resurrection. Indeed, it might be said that the descent into Hell is a dramatization of what was in fact accomplished by the Redemption. Similarly, the descent into the river and the ascent from it, com-

---

[20]"If the Acheron is meant, the ocean can rightly be said to have no vaunt over it, as it does not empty into the sea, but runs down through Hell." *Divina Commedia* ed. Grandgent, *ad loc.*

[21]Quoted and translated by Daniélou, 271, from *De Baptismo* IV, 1; *Patrologia Graeca* XII, 843A.

[22]Lundberg has demonstrated that the *abyssos* mentioned in Rom. 10:7 represents the realm of the dead: "Who shall descend into the deep? (That is, to bring up Christ again from the dead.)" This seems to be St. Paul's gloss of Deut. 30:13: "Who shall go over the sea for us . . . ." This is one scriptural passage among many adduced by Lundberg in support of his argument that the realm of the dead was represented by the waters. His second chapter is an exhaustive study of the theme of the waters of the dead associated with the Jordan. He goes on to explore in rich detail "les bases cosmologiques de l'idée du descensus dans le baptême" (64–72).

memorated by the liturgy of Baptism in the primitive church, was
read as a Baptism "unto death" of the new convert; in effect, a
Christian *descensus*. When we consider that the entrance into grace
of the newly baptized soul is completely analogous to the restoral to
grace of the fallen sinner in later Christianity, we come to see that
it is precisely as a "Jordan" that we are to read the barrier in Dante's
poem: the *fiumana* is a death which is a prelude to authentic life,
but before the barrier is surmounted, a descent in humility, into Hell
itself, will be required.

All of this was thought to be contained in the name of the river.
In an exegetical tradition that extends from Philo Judaeus to Thomas
Aquinas, the etymology of the name "Jordan" was said to be καταβασις
αὐτῶν, *descensus eorum*, "their descent."[23] Aquinas explains the
meaning of the name in terms that precisely recall the "descent into
humility" that Charles Singleton[24] has shown to be the tropological
meaning of Dante's journey through Hell: "It should be said that in
Baptism there is an ascent to the perfection of grace, which requires
a descent in humility, according to James 4:6: 'To the humble He
gives grace.' And the name of Jordan is to be referred to that type of
descent."[25] That type of descent will be required of Dante's pilgrim
before he can make his ascent to grace.

Thus far we have been concerned with ancient ideas that constitute,
at best, remote sources of the complex of motifs represented by Dante's
fiumana. Except for the passage from Aquinas, none of the authors we
have quoted were known directly to the poet. There is one ancient
expression of some of these ideas, however, that may well constitute
a more proximate source, in that it appears in Virgil. Indeed, it is so
strikingly like Dante's poetic representation that, were it from a more
familiar work, we might be tempted to suggest a direct influence. It
is, however, from the *Georgics*,[26] which Dante never quotes and
which does not appear to have been frequently mentioned in the
Middle Ages. In the fourth book, Virgil presents us with the famous

[23]Philo Judaeus, *Legum Allegoriarum* II, 22; Origen, *Commentary on St. John*,
VI, 42; thereafter a commonplace. See Daniélou, 268. Cf. St. Jerome, *Patrologia
Latina* 22, 722.

[24]"In Exitu . . .," 109.

[25]*Summa Theologiae* III, 39, art. 4 *ad* 2.

[26]For Dante's knowledge of the *Georgics*, see V. Zabughin, *Vergilio nel Rinasci-
mento Italiano* (Bologna, 1921), 10, who affirms, against Moore, *Studies in Dante*,
I (Oxford, 1896), 9 and 21, that Dante knew the *Georgics* very well.

fable of Aristaeus, the shepherd and demi-god who attempted to
violate Eurydice and so indirectly caused her death by the "solitary
shore" of a river. The fable is directly concerned with telling the
story of the punishment of Aristaeus and of his subsequent expiation.
All his bees are killed and he must descend to the abode of the gods
and wrestle with Proteus in order to discover what sacrifices must be
made before his bees can be restored to him. The story begins with
the shepherd's complaint by the "holy spring of the river-head" to
his mother Cyrene, "who dwellest here deep beneath the flood":
"why hast thou borne me in the gods' illustrious line—if indeed my
father is . . . Apollo of Thymbra—to be the scorn of doom? or whither
is thy love for me swept away?" From her chamber "in the river
depths" Cyrene hears his cry. Of great interest to us, however, is the
fact that another sea-nymph, Arethusa, hears his lament and calls
him to the attention of his mother:

O not vainly startled by so heavy a moan, Cyrene sister, he thine own,
thy chiefest care, mourning Aristaeus stands in tears by Peneus' ancestral
wave, and calls thee cruel. . . . To her the mother, stricken in soul with
fresh alarm: Lead him, quick, lead him to us; he, she cries, may unfor-
bidden tred the threshold of the gods. With that she bids the deep streams
retire, leaving a broad path for his steps to enter in. *But round him the
mountain-wave stood curving* and clasped him in its mighty fold, and
sped him beneath the river. . . .[27]

When they are finally reunited, son and mother together drink a
libation to Oceanos, "Father of all things" and ruler of this "sisterhood
of nymphs."

Dramatically speaking, the elements here bear a striking resem-
blance to what we have seen of the situation in Canto II: the
hero, about to undertake a *descensus* in expiation for a sin, is heard
weeping on the banks of a river associated with the Other World. His
cry is heard in a court of godly "sisters" who undertake a kind of
relay in order to bring him to the threshold of the gods. The most
important difference between the two dramatic representations is that

[27]*Georgics* IV, 353 ff. trans. Wm. C. McDermott (New York: Modern Library,
1950), 347 (my italics). It is interesting to observe that in the famous simile about
Glaucus, who became a consort of the gods (*Par.* I, 68), Dante is recalling the
Ovidian story in which the fisherman calls upon the sea-divinities to ask "Oceanus
and Tethys to purge [his] mortal nature all away." Here too, Oceanos is suggestive
of Jordan. For the importance of the Ovidian story for Dante's allegory, see Singleton, *Dante Studies* II: "Journey to Beatrice" (Cambridge, 1958), 28.

in Virgil's fable the shepherd actually crosses the river. It happens that this detail of the story is precisely what attracted some Christians to it and caused them to interpret it according to a much more familiar crossing. Lactantius, for example, when discussing the crossing of the Red Sea by the Jews, quotes Virgil, and specifically the lines I have italicized, in order to describe the parting of the waters: "Curvata in montis faciem circumstetit unda."[28] Even in the Renaissance, commentators on these verses recall that something similar occurred ": in exitu Israel de Aegypto."[29] Whether or not Dante knew Virgil's verses and the Christian gloss directly, they certainly are paralleled in a striking way by his own poetic representation.

All of what we have said so far has served to show the Jordan's superiority to any body of water. We have yet to explain specifically why it should be compared to a sea or indeed why the sea should be mentioned at all. But if we keep in mind the fact that river and sea should both exist on the same level of reality then the answer begins to become apparent. The only sea that can be compared to the Jordan is the Red Sea, and it happens that they exist on precisely the same levels of reality, liturgically and literally, as stages in the drama of Exodus. An examination of their relationship to each other will bring us closer to a clear understanding of Dante's verse.

We have asserted that the figure for baptism was the Israelites' crossing of the River Jordan under the leadership of Joshua. It happens, however, that this contradicts no less an authority than St. Paul. In a famous passage which enunciated the principle of figural interpretation, St. Paul suggested that it was the crossing of the Red Sea that constituted the figure:

I would not have you ignorant, brethren, that our fathers [the Israelites] were all under the cloud and passed through the sea. And all in Moses were baptized in the cloud and the sea. . . . Now all these things were done in a figure for us. (I Cor. 10:1)

---

[28]Lactantius, *De. Div. Inst.* IV, 10, mentioned by Dölger, "Der Durchzug durch den Jordan als Sinnbild der Christlichen Taufe," *Antike und Christentum* II, 71, n. 5. According to Servius (*In Georg.* IV, 373), Marius Victorinus, in a commentary now lost, interpreted the *purpureum mare* of this passage as the Red Sea. Servius was probably unaware that this reflected a reading of the passage according to Exodus. See Pierre Courcelle, "Les pères de l'eglise devant les enfers virgiliens," *Archives d'histoire doct. et litt. du Moyen Age*, 30 (1955), 70.

[29]Badius Ascensius and Iodocus Clichtoveus both make the point. See *P. Virgilii Maronis Opera*, Bonello edition (Venice, 1566), 118 (*ad loc.*)

Thereafter, the great majority of exegetes asserted that the crossing of the Red Sea was the type of baptism. According to Jean Daniélou, Origen was the innovator who established the crossing of Jordan as a more suitable figure of baptism since it represented a later stage in the journey to grace. In his commentary on John, he sought to establish a relationship between the progress of the Jews and the progress of the convert to God thus initiating the tropological reading of Exodus upon which the structure of Dante's poem depends. He may well be also the first to claim the river's superiority over the sea:

And even if those Paul speaks of were baptized in the cloud and in the sea, there is something harsh and bitter in their baptism. They are still in the fear of their enemies, crying out to the Lord and to Moses. *But the baptism in Joshua which takes place in sweet and drinkable water is in many ways superior to the earlier one.*[30]

Again, in a homily, he makes the classic division of the soul's progress to Grace in terms of the stages of Exodus:

And you who have just abandoned the darkness of idolatry . . . then it is that you begin first to leave Egypt. When you have been included in the number of the catechumens . . . you have passed over the Red Sea. And if you come to the sacred font of Baptism . . . you shall enter into the land of promise.[31]

Daniélou has remarked that the "general tradition of the Church, which saw in the crossing of the Red Sea the type of Baptism, was too strong to allow this other symbolism. . . ."[32] Nevertheless, the symbolism of Jordan as Baptism and therefore as "superior" to the Red Sea persisted at least until Thomas Aquinas, who believed he had biblical authority for this interpretation. This authority was strong enough to influence Dante's poetic representation of the drama of salvation.

When one reads the New Testament, one discovers that Christ actually baptized his followers, not in the Red Sea, but in the River

[30]*Commentary on St. John* VI, 43–44 (my italics), quoted and translated in Daniélou, 263. Philo Judaeus had already stressed the moral dimension of the drama of Exodus in *De Migratione Abrahami* 151. For Origen's reading, see Völker, *Das Vollkommenheitsideal des Origenes* (Tübingen, 1931).

[31]*Commentary on St. John* I, 3, Daniélou, 269.

[32]P. 270. Franz Dölger's hypothesis was that the crossing of the Red Sea represented merely the negative effects of Baptism, whereas the crossing of the Jordan represented the actual reception of grace. Daniélou seeks to qualify this assertion, 261.

Jordan. Moreover, one discovers that the gospels mention not one but two types of baptism: the baptism of the precursor, who for this very reason is known as John the Baptist, and the baptism of Christ, which is the true baptism. John says of himself: "I indeed baptize you with water unto repentance; but he that cometh after me is mightier than I, whose shoes I am not worthy to bear: he shall baptize you with the Holy Ghost and with fire. . . ."[33] Mediaeval exegetes and philosophers saw in the two types of baptism an opportunity to distinguish the preparation for grace from grace itself, which is to say, the repentance of the sinner from the forgiveness of sin.[34] The baptism of John came to represent repentance for a former way of life and the preparation for a new, the new life that was sacramentally represented by the baptism of Christ. Every soul therefore required a baptism of water, repentance, as well as a baptism of the Holy Ghost, that is, justification, and the principle was supported by Christ's words from the Gospel according to St. John: "Verily, verily I say unto thee, except a man be born of water *and* of the Spirit, he cannot enter into the kingdom of God." The figure of baptism in general was indeed the Red Sea; baptism in the special sense, however, as a sacrament which brought with it grace, came to be figured by the River Jordan. Aquinas distinguishes between the two types:

It should be said that the crossing of the Red Sea prefigures baptism insofar as that baptism takes away sin. But the crossing of the River Jordan insofar as it opens the gates of heaven, which is a more important effect of baptism and can be fulfilled only by Christ. It was more fitting then that Christ should be baptized in the Jordan rather than in the Sea.[35]

Again describing the figure, he insists on the supereminence of Jordan:

The River Jordan was the means whereby the children of Israel entered into the promised land. This the baptism of Christ has above all other

---

[33]Matthew 3: 11, in the Authorized Version. Thomas Aquinas insists that the baptism of John was the *baptismus poenitentiae* (Mark 1:4) and makes this statement which is essential for an understanding of what the Baptism of John represented: "nihil in illo baptismo efficiebatur quod homo facere non posset." *Summa Theologiae* III, 38, art 2. resp.

[34]Mark 1:4 was the scriptural authority for distinguishing repentance from the actual forgiveness of sin. See also Gregory the Great's insistence that the baptism of John could not forgive sin: *In. Evang.* I, hom. 7, PL 76, 1101. Also important is the figural role played by John as the frontier between Judaism and Christianity: "fuit enim terminus legis et initium evangelii" *Summa Theologiae* III, 38, art. 1 *ad* 2.

[35]*Ibid.* 39, art. 4 *ad* 1.

baptisms, that it leads into the Kingdom of God which is signified by the promised land.[36]

It is precisely because the River Jordan is a figure for the baptism of Christ that it is a river unlike all other rivers, superior to the sea, which figures only the baptism of John the Baptist. It stands to the sea as Christ stands to the Baptist, *the greatest of all prophets* (Luke 7:8). It is, in the figure of baptism, a river over which *not even the Red Sea* can boast.

Finally, in order to show how the poet's contemporaries would read both the Red Sea and the River Jordan together in a figure representing the justification of sinners, we have only to turn to St. Bonaventure. His remarks on the subject constitute a reinterpretation of Origen's exegesis not in terms of the typology of baptism, but according to the figure of conversion. Writing about the correspondence of the Jewish passover to its Christian fulfilment, Easter, the liturgical time of Dante's poem, he notices that the word *pascha* signifies *transitus*, a crossing:

There are three crossings, that is, the crossing that is a beginning [*incipientium*] and the crossing that is in the making [*proficientium*] and the crossing that is an arrival [*pervenientium*] . . . this then is the threefold paschal crossing, of which the first is through the *sea* of contrition, the second through the *desert* of religion, the third through the *Jordan* of death; and thus we arrive at the promised land.[37]

The great Franciscan Doctor then goes on to show how these three stages on the way to sanctifying (or *pervenient*) grace were foreshadowed by the three paschal feasts celebrated by the Jews, according to the account of the twelfth chapter of Exodus:

it is written that first they ate the *pasch* of the Lord and this was the crossing of the beginning, for after this feast, having left Egypt, they crossed the Red Sea. And the children of Israel also had a paschal supper in the dessert . . . at the mountain of Sinai, and that signified the crossing that was in the making, for it was while the children of Israel were progressing through the desert. They had the third paschal supper at their entry into the promised land . . . and this was the crossing of arrival for it was held in the promised land after the Jordan had been crossed.[38]

   [36]*Ibid.* art. 4 resp.

   [37]Bonaventure, *Collationes in Evangelium Joannis* XIII, coll. XLVIII *Opera* (Quaracchi) VI, 597. Probably the intermediary for this moral reading of Exodus between the Greek and the Latin tradition was Ambrose: *Hexaemeron* 1:4 (*Corpus scriptorum ecclesiasticorum latinorum*, Ambrosius I, 12.).   [38]*Ibid.*

It is clear from the words that he uses to describe these crossings (*incipientium, proficientium, pervenientium*) that Bonaventure has the moral sense of Exodus in mind, according to which, in Dante's words, the soul is "brought out of the state of misery and grief into the state of grace," which is to say, sanctifying or "pervenient" grace. Furthermore, this conception of the stages of moral development corresponds to the drama of the *Purgatorio*, from the emergence on the shore, to the ascent of the mountain, to the crossing of the river to Beatrice. Here in the prologue scene, the figural landscape prefigures the successful journey that is to come.

Bonaventure tells us that Jordan signifies death (we hear in the background the plea of Lucy—"Non vedi tu la morte che 'l combatte?") and we understand now that he refers to the death which is a prerequisite to life in the Pauline sense:

Know ye not that so many of us as were baptized into Jesus Christ were baptized into his death? Therefore we are buried with him by baptism into death: that like as Christ was raised up from the dead by the glory of the Father, even so we also should walk in newness of life. . . . (Romans 6:3–4).

On his own, Dante has survived the perils of the dark wood and thus, from the perspective of heaven, the dangerous waters of everyman's Red Sea. Again he has made some progress on the desert slope. It is the wolf that finally stops him, short of the final crossing which is death and at the same time life. He will be introduced to that *vita nuova* when he is immersed in the river Lethe at the top of Purgatory. Now, in the prologue scene, he is blocked on the shores of a *fiumana* which he cannot cross until, like Christ, he descends to the depths of the earth. The implication seems to be that the preparation for grace lies within the competence of man, in the purely natural order. However, only Beatrice can bring the pilgrim the grace that is needed to accomplish a death and resurrection. This is to state in theological terms what we have known all along: were it not for Beatrice, neither the journey nor the poem could have come into existence.

It has perhaps not occurred to Dante commentators to identify the *fiumana* with Christianity's river because Dante's river is so clearly terrifying, while the Jordan was traditionally a river of salvation. As we have said, however, this is to read the river entirely from the pilgrim's perspective and to forget that the purpose of the journey is to correct that perspective. In a Christian context, all salvation is a consequence of the death of the self. In a literary context, the poem, the triumph of the author, entails a death of the protagonist, a detachment of the self that *was* from the self that *is*. Unless one understands the death of the self involved in Dante's experience (as pilgrim and author), there is no way of appreciating the drama of the *Inferno*. The fears expressed by the pilgrim along the way constitute the very *askesis* that makes rebirth possible; if this were not so, they would have to be dismissed as an example of dramatic coyness on the part of a man who knows from the beginning that everything will turn out all right. It would be as if we refused to believe that the Dostoevskian hero is really frightened by the firing squad, when we know from the existence of the story that the reprieve from the Czar came through. Dante's river of death represents exactly the same sort of limit situation. Short of the barrier, progress is impossible; beyond it, there seems to be only extinction. The story is testimony of the fact that this extinction of a false self in an inverted world is a necessary step before authentic life, and the story, can be born.

As readers of the story, we cannot know the experience of a death and resurrection. It is for this reason that the story was written: as a confession of faith for other men. The best we can do is to accept the *exemplum*, the story itself, in good faith and as part of our own experience, much as Dante accepted Virgil's story, as a preparation for a synthesis of which his author could know nothing at all. If, in the twentieth century, it seems unlikely that a Beatrice will come or, were she to come, that we should call her Sanctifying Grace, the fault is neither ours nor Dante's; we shall at least have walked together to the river.

The Living Poet
and the Myth of Time:
Christian Comedy

JOHN F. MAHONEY

IT WOULD BE a fairly easy matter to begin this, or any other, attempt at a new evaluation of Dante's artistic accomplishment by assuming that the *Commedia* is *the* great poem in western literary history. Any scholar, on the other hand, would much prefer to have his readers come to this conclusion as a result of his argument. As bromidic an introductory remark as this may seem to be, it is a necessary one. Students of Dante, as has often been remarked, have been cheered by his emergence from the age of pedantic scholarship. In the twenty years which have preceded this anniversary of the poet's birth, they have been encouraged to begin new estimates of Dante's artistry as it is notably displayed in his greatest poem, the *Commedia*, and encouraged also to turn to a more literary and less historical study of the minor works. If there were any difficulties to be foreseen it would be because all the historical study was not completed, however long it seemed to have been going on, when the "new criticism" of Dante began.

The burden of what I have had to say previously about the *Commedia*, and about the structure of the *Purgatorio* in particular, has been, if it is rightly assembled, to indicate the artistic importance in Dante's plan of the historical evidence for the theme of the "Second Adam."[1] The availability to the poet of the Victorine-Augustinian

[1] "The Role of Statius and the Structure of *Purgatorio*," 79th *Annual Report of the Dante Society of America* (Boston, 1961), 11–37.

tradition of Incarnational theology, and the apparent dominance of that tradition in his construction of the *Purgatorio*, alter considerably the function of that *cantica* in the whole art of his poem. The impact on man of return to his own point of origin, as it is sketched especially by Gregory of Nyssa,[2] adds to Dante, as central character in his own poem, a dimension which the more conventional protagonist readings could not develop. The basic and dualistic distinction between *stasis* and *kinesis*, which are seen as the controlling characterizations of the three regions of the afterlife, reduce the historical, theological, and, perhaps, exegetical divisions of the *Commedia* to two, even while the structural plan of the poem employs three. There are, after all, only two states in which man can be: alive or dead. This is a distinction, drawn from an earthly point of view, from one which is spiritually meaningful. Man is either kinetic, subject to change, to improvement or to decline, or he is static—his changeability, his subjectability to improvement or to deterioration over. There are no mortal souls, except the poet himself, to be found among the figures in the *Commedia*, but there are some who are still alive. These are the spirits whom Dante meets in Purgatory, souls still kinetic, still changing. From Gregory's sub-distinction, we learn too that they are in a state of *prokope*, not of *tenos*, that their return to Adam's pristine state is guided, not erratic as it had been while they were on earth and still mortal. The uncertain and often failing motions of man have disappeared. They proceed, as Dante describes them, with the innocent confidence of the child, blown only by trustworthy winds, rested in their sleep, not anxious about their progress or speed. Significantly, they grow anxious with fear only at the prospect of Adam's original act, the scene which they must witness once (as Dante understands it), as they visit the Valley of Princes. The type of *stasis* they will reach is assured; it is the *stasis* of Paradise. One ought not to overlook the contrast so deliberately to be drawn from Dante's *terze rime* descriptions of these two states of *stasis*, the one spiritually replete, the other hopeless, but both drawn in the firm image of the Trinity of the God. In the *Inferno* we read from famous lines:

> Per me si va nella città dolente
> Per me si va nell' etterno dolore,
> Per me si va tra la perduta gente.

---

[2]*Ibid.*, 13.

Giustizia mosse il mio alto fattore:
   Fecemi la divina potestate,
   La somma sapienza e 'l primo amore.

Dinanzi a me non fuor cose create
   Se non etterne, e io etterna duro.
   Lasciate ogni speranza, voi ch' entrate.   (*Inf*. III, 1-9)

Against "power, wisdom, and love," are contrasted the fixed qualities
of these spirits: woe, pain, and abandonment. The allusion here to
the Trinity has been commonly compared to the perverse allusion of
the triple head of Satan at the end of the *Inferno*, a symmetry appropriate at the end of the given *cantica*.[3] Of more interest, perhaps, but
of less renown, is the contrast to this famous inscription over the
gate which is presented at the end of all three *cantiche*:

. . . "Noi siamo usciti fore
   del maggior corpo al ciel ch'è pura luce:

luce intellettual, piena d'amore;
   amor di vero ben, pien di letizia;
   letizia che trascende ogni dolzore.   (*Par*. XXX, 38-42)

Both of these eternal regions, Hell and Paradise, are in *stasis*,
although the one is of beatitude and the other of hopelessness. This
contrast makes the relationship between Purgatory and the other two
states an unequal one. The poem is not composed of three logical
stages, whatever it may be on the level of narrative structure. *Tenos*,
the state of mortal man still awaiting death, is, in a certain sense,
equally related to both Hell and Paradise from the perspective of
Incarnational theology, and if no account is taken of the modification
of that view—which will be explained later—by the theology of Atonement. But, except for Dante, there are no mortal men in the *Commedia*; all those who are there are at least dead. The distinction among
them is only the particular state of death, so to speak, that they are
in. Those in Purgatory, while they have passed the barrier of death,
have not yet proceeded to the *stasis*, which they seek. Instead, the
tenos has been turned to *prokope*, an ordered progress analogous only
to the life of man by original Divine intention, before the Fall. That
they seek to return to man's state before the Fall, to pre-Adamite

[3]*Inf.*, XXXIV.

existence, is due to the inalterable reality of the nature of existence: "The end is always the same as the beginning."[4]

The foregoing should help establish the relationship which exists between Dante and the spirits in Purgatory. Like them, he is alive to the extent that his spirit is still in *kinesis*. Like them, he is in search of the *stasis* which all men, in this view, are said to seek. He stands, like them, in direct contrast to the spirits in Hell and in Paradise, in horrified contrast to the former, and in envying contrast to the latter. Although as man still mortal, one who has not yet experienced death, his proper state of *kinesis* is that of *tenos*, even on the basis of logical limitations of this analysis—*stasis* vs. *kinesis, kinesis* being either *tenos* or *prokope*—his relationship with the spirits of Purgatory is an essentially greater one than it could be with the spirits whom he watches in Hell, and, it must be added, greater than it could be with the spirits whom he sees in Paradise. It is therefore of much significance that Dante, although he is in the regions ascribed to each *cantica*, participates only with those in Purgatory. There is a carefully maintained perspective of distance between the poet and the spirits in Hell and between the poet and the spirits in Paradise. He is clearly the watcher, the intruder into these two worlds, whereas in the *Purgatorio* he experiences all the events and all the varying durations of stay on the ledges. He goes through the nights and the days; he witnesses the controlled panic of the recurring temptation scene in the garden. Finally, he emerges through the purifying fire of the top of the mountain to the qualified but pristine perfection of Adam. Similarly, his reaction to the Pageant of the Church Militant is an active one and an emotionally responsive one. Although he accomplishes perfection in Purgatory through the *prokope* which is the measured order toward praeternatural perfection, unlike the spirits he will not continue to the assortment of *stases* in Paradise, but will instead retreat to be the removed watcher there which he was in Hell.

That is why the role of Statius, as I hope I have shown in my earlier article, is not only significant, but of the first importance among those of the guides, although this is not to suggest that Statius ought to assume literary importance over Virgil and Beatrice, but rather the importance of a *sine qua non* among the guides for the poet, for

[4]"The Role of Statius," 36.

Dante, or for whomever Dante is surrogate. For the real inhabitants of the regions of the *Commedia*, both Virgil and Beatrice are irrelevant as guides. Those in Hell have nothing to do with Virgil. He is simply, as the opening cantos tell us, Dante's guide. In Paradise Divine Will ranks the spirits, as La Pia tells us;[5] until he reaches her Beatrice is less a guide for Dante than a motive. But Statius, on the other hand, is symbolically the direct guide in Purgatory not only of Dante, and of the true spirits of the region, but eventually of Virgil as well. We have seen his aptness for this role in the symbolic existence, not of the historical Statius, but of the Statius Dante chose to describe, in the ancient poet's tenure of life in both the pre-Redemptive and the post-Redemptive worlds. If it is possible that literary sentiment keeps us from preferring Statius to Virgil, it is important at least to note that Dante is quick to recognize the preferability of relying on Statius over Virgil as Purgatorial guide, and that Virgil himself welcomes Statius' ascendency to that task.

It seems necessary then, in view of the foregoing argument, to take as a premise that the beginning of understanding in the reading of the *Commedia* lies in the *Purgatorio*. The difficulty with the various dramatic readings of the poem which have appeared in the past twenty years[6] is that they aim at reproducing for the reader what is essentially an aesthetic experience and therefore incapable of such reproduction. Against the context of the various "journies to the underworld," both classical and Christian-mythological, which preceded Dante, the *Commedia* is read as by far the best of these fictional visions. If the preferred precedent is classical, the poem then becomes an experience in self-study. Out of such readings have come the extrapolations on literary autobiography which characterize the work of Fergusson, for example, and even parts of Gilson's exposition. In this type of reading,[7] the value of the poem in the history of ideas is refracted into an image of a great and sensitive individual, whose

---

[5]*Par.* III, 85.

[6]There is no great value in citing specific critics: in part, these readings stem from an effect of the New Criticism, and should be given the credit of having revived literary interest in Dante in much the same manner in which they revived literary interest in other works. On the other hand, Dante has suffered as much as other works have from historical misreading.

[7]Such as Irma Brandeis, *Ladder of Vision* (London, 1960).

monument to his own mind was vested in the tradition of the mytho-
graphic vision of the afterlife.

If, on the other hand, the preferred precedent is Christian, and
perhaps even Pauline, certain contrary readings develop. Many critics,
following the lead of Wicksteed—Mandonnet, for one—extract from
Dante's complex art the more distilled intention of scholastic continuity.[8] This view, appealing especially to both opponents in the post-
Lutheran debates, was able to support the positions of the orthodox
scholastic mind as well as the dissident evangelical theologian. Thus
the *Commedia* has been made to seem either a basically personal portrayal of a sensitive man's view of history and historical individuals,
or it has been taken as the perfect "mediaeval cathedral" of scholastic
thought.

One could say of these kinds of reading that they describe a kind
of school of criticism by themselves, but only along with the whole
bibliography of attempts to reclaim, as it were, the monuments of
literature for contemporary preference. An illustration may be in
point, and one can be drawn from the history of interpretations of
Elizabethan tragedy. It is no doubt a further evidence of Shakespeare's
enduring art that his plays can be seen as so many kinds of tragedy,
and that, for many, it would be unbearable to have to read his work
within the framework of either the mediaeval Christian theory of
tragedy or the Senecan-revenge tradition. Still, whatever may be
debated about Shakespeare's own intentions in writing tragedy, his
plays are re-read and re-interpreted continually as modern tragedy;
one may cite extremes which range from the nineteenth-century
revisions to the productions of Margaret Webster.

In a sense, this has happened to Dante as well. It is aesthetically
interesting and itself a further evidence of Dante's enduring art that
his *Commedia* can be read as a marvel of Christian myth, or as an
early Joycean introversion of the mind of the artist. But it is critically
unsound to substitute the elasticity of the art for the substance of
Dante's own artistic intention. Such substitutions have led to the
obvious preference we have for the "mythologizable" narrative of the
Inferno, and to the undue emphasis which has been placed on the

---

[8]Such as K. T. Swing, *The Fragile Leaves of the Sybil* (Westminster, Md.:
The Newman Press, 1962).

importance of Reason in the allegory. One aspect of Dante's praise of Virgil does place the latter above all others, but this poetic attraction Virgil has for Dante cannot be extended from its source in the *Inferno* into a governing intentional structure for the other two *cantiche*. The fact that the *Inferno* alone is read by more people makes it possible to remark that most of these read Dante with no awareness at all of his artistic intention. Almost all readers of Dante, then, become appreciative of his work from a rationalistic preference; his contribution to the history of literature is that of an extraordinary narrative, an incident in the history of imaginative art, some mythology of a forgotten and irrelevant age.

My studies of Incarnational theology, especially the history of this doctrine from the patristic to mediaeval times, and the special relevance which changing concepts about the doctrine have to mediaeval tragedy, all convinced me some time ago that the extension of Dante's theme was historical more than eschatalogical. That is, the source of all that structures the *Commedia* is the history of doctrine, and within that history the doctrine of the Incarnation. How ever the characterizing detail of the poem is absorbed in the underworld or the afterlife, the theme of the poem has relatively little to do with either. Nor is the poem explained by remarking on the importance of Dante's experience to Dante the man, or to mankind. Such a moral artistic purpose is more automatic than it is intentional or sufficient.

On the other hand, to discuss the detail of Dante's choices as appropriate is unsatisfactory. By such analysis, the time of his journey, for example, the weekend of Holy Week, and the host of other Christian reminiscences, have as sufficient aesthetic explanation only the neatness of their importance in Christian tradition or lore. They are, so to speak, the Christian equivalences of the references a non-Christian poet might have made (and did make) to his own cosmological mythology.

What must be said here instead is that the purpose of Dante's work, even as he described it in the closing lines of the *Vita Nuova*,[9] was less a fictionalized version, however religiously centred, of a trip to the underworld, a trip made in the tradition of the Classical as well as the Christian poet, than it was a dramatization of the Christian

[9]*Vita Nuova*, XLII.

belief in Atonement. However the paradox resounds, it is this: that in spite of the severely rational structuring of the whole poem, the poetic experience for both writer and reader is essentially non-rational. That is, whoever reads the work with any affection must do so having in mind a firm premise which is basically a theological one. This premise, whether it is credible as doctrine or as mere lore, is that the world was "redeemed." All of the metaphorical existences which comprise the cantos of the poem are only comparable to human experience by analogy. Or again, all the inhabitants of the regions of the poem, whether static now or still in the *prokope* of *kinesis*, are proof of the world's redemption, whereas those who live must still, if they are Christian, operate on that assumption which is drawn from faith alone.

The reason for this remarkable underlying reality—and one may speak with some assurance, considering the far more elaborate and essential role it plays in the *Commedia* than it does, say, in the *Aeneid* —is that the traditional relationship between the theologies of the Incarnation and of the Atonement had come under contest in this era of the Middle Ages. We have remarked elsewhere[10] the central position in the Christian notion of tragedy held by the theology of the Second Adam. And as it was suggested there that there is no document which indicates this importance more clearly than does the *Exultet* of Easter Week, or Holy Saturday in particular, here one may also point to a famous text from that cycle, the *Victimae Paschalis*. The point of the Easter liturgy, restored or unrestored, has always been to re-dramatize, once through the mime of *tenebrae*, and at another and perhaps better time through the Easter midnight vigil, the whole record of human experience in regard to Fall and Redemption. But beyond the significance of the Second Adam as the testament to the justice of man's hopeful wait for restoration is the importance of his conduct as Atoner for the weight of the first sin. This importance is that of a victor, as the other relevant hymn, *Christus Victor*, reminds us.[11] It may be asserted immediately then that the choice of Easter Week by Dante for the temporal location of his essentially extra-temporal progression was neither fond nor merely appropriate; it

[10]"Chaucerian Tragedy and the Christian Tradition," *Annuale Mediaevale* III, pp. 81–99.
[11]See E. Kantorowicz, *Laudes Regiai* (Berkeley, 1958).

was obviously not the sentimental choice of the Christian for whom these days were the most important in the year. Rather, that choice was inescapable as he, as mankind seen from the perspective of the drama of the human experience of sin and Atonement, was to dramatize further the significance of both the Incarnation of the Second Adam and of his role as Atoner. The *selva oscura* in which Dante finds himself, as he tells us in the opening canto, is the *maggior corpo* from which he emerges in Canto XXX of the *Paradiso*. The world of the living, how ever it be redeemed and Christian, is an obscure one and dependent on acceptance of doctrine for its own assurance of that redemption. The purpose of theological discussion of this subject from the days of the earliest Fathers to Dante's time had been to vivify and to make concrete the detail of that inarticulable acceptance.

The earliest perhaps, Iranaeus, stresses the reality of the bonds with which Adam's sin had tied man, and explains the Incarnation as the necessary step by which God could descend to man to free him from sin and death. Eventually the bond becomes "sin, death and the devil," but the exposition is still, by many years, pre-legal in its detail. Augustine accepts and extends this "Classic" idea of Atonement. Neo-Platonically, he sees the inevitability of God's act, as well as its explanation as a historical fact, as an irrepressible extension of God's love for his creatures, a love which survives even the nature of the Fall. Especially notable is the fact that Augustine saw the Atonement in the same kind of dramatic context in which Christianity was to see it for centuries to come, remarkable enough in the art and purposes of the mystery cycles,[12] but even more remarkably portrayed in the drama of the *Commedia*. One may point to Gregory the Great, perhaps, as the figure who first gave, in a well-known way, vital dimension to the figures in the drama, the vital dimension we find continued and perfected artistically in the character of Satan in the ninth circle of Hell.

For those who first made expositions of these theological issues, or, as it may be summed, the *Cur Deus Homo* theme, the development of this Classical theory of Atonement was an unconscious growth. But it is significant that sin plays far less a role in their explanations

---

[12]A forthcoming book by O. B. Hardison, Jr. (to appear from the Johns Hopkins University Press), discusses at length the drama of theology represented by these plays.

than it did in those of the theologians just prior to Luther, and against whom, in fact, part of Luther's rebellion was directed. The comprehension of death and the establishment of some workable relationship between death, which Redemption had symbolically but not physically conquered, and the devil were more immediately necessary goals. So the stress of the earliest writings is on the movement of God toward man and back again, as he accomplished his Atonement to and for himself. The fact that in the Resurrection Christ had conquered death became counsel for the tremulous believer, because, though death could pose the physical threat to all men which it was promised it would in the canonical apochryphal writings on the events of Genesis, mankind could be assured that death's sting had been removed. Or, as a later poet put it: "After the first death, there is no other."[13] The effect of this surely was to place the Resurrection secondary to the impact of the Incarnation and Atonement, an attitude which prevailed until the arrival of a more legalistic age, and one whose growth of concern for rational efficiency drew the doctrine of Resurrection into a central focus.

There is no particular need here to elaborate on the character of the Latin theory of Atonement, since the history of this, as well as the theological history of the entire subject, has been explored frequently, if not always well.[14] Moreover, it was not for but against the Latin doctrine that Dante wrote, as we hope to show below. Yet to recall the role which Anselm played in this development may be important. While few theologians have been more widely misinterpreted, it is true that out of his celebrated *Cur Deus Homo?* came the seeds of the "Abuse of Power" theory of redemption, and the doctrine of man's obligation to atone to God for his race's fall.[15] He explains the humanity of Christ thereby, but he led the way to the emphasis on sin, a basic pessimism in regard to man's attempts to achieve his own perfection, and what has been regularly seen as an exaggerated importance and mobility attributed to the Devil.

---

[13]Dylan Thomas, "A Refusal to Mourn the Death by Fire of a Child in London."

[14]The opening pages of Gustaf Aulen's *Christus Victor* (New York, 1931) provide a fair survey.

[15]This is a doctrine which seems to have had significant literary influence. See especially Timothy Fry, O.S.B., "The Unity of the Ludus Coventriae," *Studies in Mediaeval Culture Dedicated to G. R. Coffman, Studies in Philology* XLVII, 527–570.

Anselm's followers, unlike the followers of the Classic theory, diminished the significance of Christ's defeat of death, and presented death instead as the final expiation, an imitation of the redeeming act of Christ, which was necessary for all men's salvation. As Aulen remarks, for Anselm the Incarnation existed as a fixed dogma in the premises of his thought, and not as a dramatic reality which, along with the Atonement, was continually effective in the world and on mankind.[16] That is to say, while in the Classic explanation of Atonement, the essential and all-requiring action of redemption was accomplished yet continually going on until the disappearance of death at the end of time, in the Latin theory, to which tradition Anselm belongs, the principle of redemption had been established and a pattern had been set for Christians to follow toward their own realization of it and participation in it. To make the contrast clearer: in the Classic theory, mankind had been redeemed, but was consigned, through the course of the world's span of existence, to live, conscious of the need to go through death, but confident of the removal of human guilt and of the defeat of the Devil. In the Latin view, the world was redeemed, but men had to accomplish their own salvation, remove their own guilt, and guard against a defeated but vengeful Devil.

The contrast is vast, when all the implications are considered. The figure of Christ changed—although with much help from the mendicants, all of whom held the Latin theory—from that of a triumphant incarnated God into that of a suffering man who was also God. Just as the eschatology of the Patristic age, vital as it was to both the social and artistic lives of early Christians, had been forgotten, so too the confidence of a redeemed Christianity sank into oblivion. Substituted for the Fathers' view of a redeemed people waiting, albeit prematurely, the end of time, was the mediaeval view of the perfect society hampered only by recalcitrant men. The emphasis on love, arising from the Neo-Platonic tradition and common to Christian understanding from Paul to Augustine and beyond, gave way to a legal interpretation of merits which, arising from the infinite act of the Redeemer, were held in escrow for men's good deeds. Such an analogy for the rapport between Redeemer and the redeemed developed rapidly. Not only do the concept of satisfaction and merit derive from this legalistic view, but

[16]Aulen, 87.

so also did the natively Latin notion of excessive merit, or supererogatory deeds and merit, and with both of these, the logic of transferability from one to another. In short, the relationship between Incarnation and Atonement was essential in the Classic theory, while it was basic to the Latin one that these two doctrines not be so related. The explanation of the Incarnation, the *Cur Deus Homo?*, is that it made the Atonement more noble, and probably more likely, since no man could be found to perform the action of redress which, in the Latin theory, man had to perform. The death of Christ, the basis of the Atonement, whose effect would exist as long as time, became too central in the Latin view, too central, at least to allow to continue the sense of triumph over sin, death, and the Devil which is conveyed in the concept of *Christus Victor*. The fact that the Eastern and Western Churches adopted a different form of the crucifix is silent evidence to this change, religious sentiment one way or the other notwithstanding. The impact of *parousia* and *etimasia*, the second coming and the sense of patient preparedness for that coming, waned, until by the day of Dante they had disappeared almost altogether. The characteristic double-effect of the Classic theory, to use Aulen's term,[17] whereby the Atonement was God's act presented to God, was foreign to Latin interpretations, and instead there grew into focus the human aspect of Christ's nature and action, necessary to the analogous demand placed on man.

Another way of examining those contrasting viewpoints, and the effect they had on the culture of the mediaeval Christian world, is in terms of the nature of time. By the age of Thomas Aquinas, who appears to follow Anselm's explanation, the threefold distinction of *stasis, kinesis*, and *tenos* or *prokope*, had disappeared. In addition, those prescriptive and legal analyses which began in the pedagogy of Augustine, charts of relationships between the vices and virtues, the beatitudes, and the sentences of the *Pater Noster*, and so on, had become the basis for logical validity in the new Aristotelian tradition. I have pointed this out at some length in the essay on "Statius and the Structure of Purgatory," noting that the misunderstanding over the hierarchy of vice and virtue, as well as over the omission of the beatitude on the meek, had obscured Statius' importance to the

[17]P. 77

poem.[18] Of more significance here is to recall that the view which Dante seems to have employed is to be found in the Augustinian tradition which was maintained in the School of the Victorines.

Augustine had observed that time was said to have been noticed because of the movement of objects.[19] He asserted, however, that it did not exist in place but in space, which seems to be a suggestion that it exists as creature, a notion germane to ages before him. By the time of the mediaeval scholastics, however, time had become a relative entity, one which was defined as the "measurement of motion," and one which has to be ascribed, as it always was, to the category of "accidental" in the Aristotelian analytics. It may be said, indeed, that relevant for this discussion, the basic difference in the concept lies in this fact that, if we use Aristotelian terms (which, of course, Dante did while Augustine did not), time was a substance for the early philosophers, and an "accident" for the mediaeval scholastics. It would have been more or less impossible for an eschatologically minded Father, conscious of the world's redemption and of the approach of *parousia*, to have understood time as an accident, potentially infinite, without any determining force on creation, and subject to the existence of the created world for its conceivability. On the contrary, he would have held that time was the basic creature in which the created world existed. It was, moreover, related to eternity in exactly the manner in which *stasis* is related to *kinesis*. The world's existence, mutable as it is, once fallen, now restored, depended on time. All that was in time was subject to change; all that was in eternity was changeless. Time was, as it were, the womb in which a world waited to be born, as it would be, on some redemptively certain day, into the true life of eternity. Meantime the world waits—one may almost say, *nella selva oscura*, subject to only partially controllable change. Its ability to control change at all, lost with the Fall, was restored with the Atonement. But its character remains the same. Hugh of St. Victor says "Tempus notat mutabilitatem."[20]

The burden of what I have said about the structure of Purgatory becomes relevant here. For just as in the search for the purpose behind the use of Statius in the poem it became evident that there was an

[18]"The Role of Statius," 25–31.
[19]*Patrologia Latina* St. Augustine I, 825–826.
[20]*Patrologia Latina* Hugh of St. Victor I, 206.

essential difference between Purgatory and the other two regions of
the poem, so it becomes evident now that the Classic theory of Atonement was the frame of reference in which Dante conceived his work
intellectually. It is evident, indeed, that the course of the poem is a
drama of the effects of Redemption. No single individual whom Dante
meets, even the pre-Christian pagans, is unmindful of the fact that
his state differs from what it was or what it might have been in the
stasis which existed before the Atonement. The poem, in this respect,
may be said to be of Christian reference not only because of the
appearance of Christians in Hell, or because of the fact that the
"opened gates of Heaven" made Paradise inhabitable again, but
because of the fact that nothing in the regions of *stasis* goes untouched
by the Atonement, everything is made better or worse accordingly.

Moreover, the poem is based on the premise of death for all, except,
of course, the privileged narrator-pilgrim who is not in the poem in
this sense. The central issue which plagued the Fathers who held the
Classic doctrine of Atonement, the problem of physical death, as a
premise to the actions of the poem, becomes a testimony, through the
drama of the effects of Atonement, to the real effect which Christ's
symbolic victory had on physical death, testifying to the truth which
these men attempted to express—that "after the first death, there is no
other." One need only contrast the characterization of Satan in Dante's
poem with his characterization elsewhere to discover how intense the
poet's effort was to underscore the Devil's immobility, his concentrated
and limited area of influence. The growing re-interpretation of him
by the Latin tradition transformed him from his comic proportions in
the mystery plays—reflected by Dante in the realm of the barrators—
into the frightening and powerful figure of the morality plays, and
of Marlowe's *Faustus* in particular. Finally, it must be observed that
Dante's stress on sin is comparatively slight. The spirits in Hell and
in Paradise are where they are, as the poem says again and again,
because of either recalcitrance or correspondence of will. While the
Latin theologian was easily able to transform this emphasis on will
into an analysis of guilt, it is the emphasis itself that is important. To
look to the *Purgatorio* for a moment, we are reminded of the fact that
when Dante has risen to the top of Purgatory, and is ready for the
curious lessons of the Pageant of the Church Militant, Virgil describes
his situation in terms of his will:

> libero, dritto e sano è tuo arbitrio,
> e fallo fora non fare a suo senno:
> per ch'io te sovra te corono e mitrio.   (*Purg.* XXVII, 140–142)

This is elucidated by Hugh of St. Victor:

. . . . Liberum arbitrium est habilitas rationalis voluntatis, qua potest, vel adjuvante gratia, ad bonum quod non habet, aut minus habet proficere; vel sinente gratia (justitia), a bono quod vel habet vel habere debet, per semetipsam deficere. Item liberum arbitrium est in rationali voluntate, spontaneus appetitus boni, qui nec coacto dare, nec invito auferri potest.[21]

The meaning of free will here is still short of the scholastic definition, as it is also in Dante's use of the term. It is *freed* will, a will made rational in its actions by the Atonement, an effect accomplished fully only at the top of the mount of Purgatory.

Again, it may be remarked pointedly that all of Dante's references to the Redeemer derive from the tradition of the *Christus Rex*.[22] Most notable, it seems, is the description in Canto XXX of the *Paradiso*, but the maliciously parodistic *Vexilla Regis* of Canto XXXIV of *Inferno* is of equal, although paradoxical, importance. One must especially recall Virgil's recollection of Christ's descent, which, in the Classic theory, was the extreme of God's deliverance of himself to himself before his return:

> ma certo poco pria se ben discerno
> che venisse colui che la gran preda
> levò a Dite del cerchio superno,
>
> da tutte parti l'alta valle feda
> tremò sì, ch'i' pensai che l'universo
> sentisse amor . . . .   (*Inf.* XII, 37–42)

That the universe "felt love" at the act of Atonement is the heart of the Classic theory.

Lastly, it is to be remarked that the Pageant of the Church Militant which Dante must witness at the end of his ascent of Purgatory, and which is part of the process to be undergone by all the *purgandi*, is less prophetic than it is recapitulative. In a sense, for those whose earthly lives are behind them, it is a memory of that life, one dominated by the ineffectuality of Christians and Christian institutions

---

[21]Hugh of St. Victor III, 574.
[22]Kantorowicz, *op. cit.*

at accommodating Atonement. But all these, like Dante, will emerge "rifatto . . . puro e disposto a salire alle stelle."[23]

We may return now to the question of artistic purpose in the poem, leaving the theological analysis behind, if, hopefully, more secure in it. My arguments as to the doctrinal basis of the structure of Dante's poem seem to implicate more than his use of Statius in the *Purgatorio* as a symbol and guide for the perfecting souls. They indicate instead that the *Purgatorio* is the key to the whole poem, describing the region whose real similarity to the live world of Dante and his readers was to lead them toward comprehension of the nature of *stasis*, both rewarded and condemned. Dante's characterization of Purgatory seems strange to orthodox tradition now, but it must have seemed innovative to the readers of his day. For the very greatest omission in the Purgatory from a modern viewpoint is that of punishment, penance, or suffering, but it is only possible to see it as an omission within the framework of a doctrine of Atonement in the Latin-Anselmine tradition. In the history of such things, Dante in fact gave more ironic impetus to the doctrine of Purgatory than perhaps any other writer. For him, as for the whole tradition of the Classic theory, Purgatory, to the extent it would have concerned them, had to be a middle region of perfectible life after death which would explain the continuance of mortality in a redeemed world, and which would, at the same time, localize the promises of accomplished Atonement. It was in Purgatory, the new franchise on happiness which Atonement had established, that what men had been denied in a fallen world could now be gained. If the world, for all the effect of Redemption on its people, remained, as it must, unreconstructed, then the necessity of God's plan for Atonement called for another region for his creation. While before, in the Judaic tradition, only Hell and Paradise existed, Christianity developed Purgatory. It is significant that in Dante's art the doctrine becomes an example of the Divine economy on which he so often remarks. Purgatory was created physically at the impact of a falling Satan, and it would end with the end of the world.

As such, Purgatory, in Dante's mind an extension of this life, is inhabited not only by souls perfecting themselves, confident in *prokope* of the direction suggested to them, but by souls gaining

[23]*Purg.* XXXIII, 145.

libero arbitrio. And Purgatory is in time, as is the rest of the created world. It is itself subject to mutability as are those who, being in it, are also in time; and it is eventually destined to disappear. If the figures in the *Inferno* and the *Paradiso* are, as I have remarked elsewhere,[24] only fine objective correlatives from the order of time extended into the order of *stasis* or eternity—where the description of the moments in which Dante chooses to see them becomes an eternal immutability—then the figures of the *Purgatorio* are defined by change and by passing. As the essence of tragedy in the Christian tradition can be seen, in terms of the *Exultet*, as the need for each man to recapitulate in manner low or high the crisis of the fall of Adam, here in the *Purgatorio* this encounter with the old story of Adam's fall, though it inspires fear, is restored, in a world whose Atonement is complete, to the comedy of which it is an integral part. This re-witnessing and eventual freedom from the onus of Adam's act is permitted, or demanded, only of those in Purgatory. For the rest, it remains the muddle of the uncertain racial or individual guilt of Hell or the beneficent amnesia of those who have passed the river Lethe. Dante's single intention in the characterization of the inhabitants of Purgatory is to show them as men still in time, still progressing, still in need for progress, but, under the effect of Atonement and in the region which Atonement made, confident both of the reality of that act and of their own eventual salvation.

The artistic basis for this accomplishment is a mythopoetic of time. Nothing so underlies Dante's poem as does his use of time, his dependence on his own understanding of it, not as a relative measurement, but as a created being, and a being whose greatest limitations were converted by the Atonement into its greatest assets. Consequently, to see the *Commedia* as a three-part narrative progression presented as a drama of exploration is to miss the point. The

---

[24]I have touched on this in "The Role of Statius." Yet the point is that the appearance of certain figures in Dante's poem cannot be taken as a projection by him about their eternal states, only about their temporal states as he or as common knowledge saw them. They cannot be said to have been "put" into Hell, for example, because Dante used them in his poem; what can be said is that what the world knew of them was such that their characters became sufficient objective correlatives for Dante's artistic communication. He seems to support this by going out of his way in the case of Guido and Buonconte to have their "places" in the afterlife come as a surprise: i.e. against the objective correlative which common knowledge of their lives established for them.

physical requirements both of the drama and of the topography and
geography of the poem's structure give physical continuity to Dante's
experience. But, to the extent that the poem is an exposition in
dramatic form of the effect of the Redemption, it can only be a two-
part poem and the parts may be defined according to varying points
of view; of salvation or of its loss, of *stasis* or of *kinesis*, of time or of
eternity. The poem as a whole as well as all of its parts is enveloped
in this mythography; every movement in it, every construction of
character, is contingent on time. The elaborate mechanism of the
time loss and time gain between Hell and Paradise, and over Purgatory, should be evidence in itself. It was not for the limitation of
human credibility that Dante chose to embrace an awkward time
sequence, accomplishing all his journey within the last days of Holy
Week. Obviously he could have shortened the time allotted along his
way, and his sense of symmetry, as we know it, would seem to have
suggested that to him. Indeed, the only reason he chose the artifice
of time gain as he moved from one region to the other was to create
a metaphor for the fact which understood as doctrine—that Purgatory,
the device by which Atonement was to have its effect, was an unexpected and unprovided-for loop in the *continuum* of time. In a
sense, living man or living poet still lived in Purgatory in a manner
which had not been provided originally, and to an extent he had not
expected or deserved. If Good Friday was the moment of tragic
recapitulation, and Easter Sunday the triumph of Resurrection, the
significance of both for mankind was in the Purgatory of Holy Saturday, the day of silence after the apparent tragedy and before the
victory. (Nor is it of small importance that under the influence of the
Latin theory, which found the gratuity of such a Purgatory impossible
because of its own penitential spirit, the liturgy of Christian faiths
moved the moment of triumph from Easter to Holy Saturday noon,
until recent restoration.)

Under this analysis, Dante's poem becomes even more understand-
ably the monument to Beatrice, as Revelation or Theology, that the
final promise of the *Vita Nuova* committed it to be. It was, in a sense,
what no man had ever spoken before, and it was sufficient to raise this
poet to the ranks of the five to whom he became the sixth. His concern
was not with the dead, the realm of those who had passed the limit
of this hopeful mutability, but with those who were still in time,

still subject to that effectual change which the Atonement promised either here or in the twilight hereafter of Purgatory. This is the time of which Hugh speaks when he says it denotes mutability. But of peculiar relevance also is Hugh's affirmation that "tempus est numerus mortuorum ordine sibi succedentium."[25] For Dante, whose purpose, taken from the Victorine tradition, was the exposition of the meaning of Redemption to a world of the living, time was very much "the number of the dead, in the order in which they succeed each other." His art was plain; it was the obverse, but at the same time the confirmation of the notion of Christian tragedy, of its ultimate irrelevance, as Troilus, for example, remarks.[26] His intention was to portray the reality of man's hope as a redeemed people for the comic resolution of the historic flaws of Adam's race. His technique, which I have seen as the use of time, accords with his own advice:

> Filosofia, mi disse, a chi la 'ntende,
> nota non pur in una sola parte
> come natura lo suo corso prende
>
> da divino intelletto e da sua arte;
> e se tu ben la tua Fisica note,
> tu troverai, non dopo molte carte,
>
> che l'arte vostra quella, quanto pote,
> segue, come 'l maestro fa il discente;
> sí che vostr'arte a Dio quasi è nepote.   (*Inf.* XI, 97–105)

Indeed, considering all this, Dante's poem is God's grandchild.

[25]Hugh of St. Victor III, 574.
[26]*Troilus and Criseyde* V, 1821–1841.

Dante's Three Communities: Mediation and Order

JOSEPH ANTHONY MAZZEO

THE DIVINA COMMEDIA is a journey from misery to bliss, from illusion and ignorance to perfect love and knowledge, from clamour to peace, and from slavery to freedom. As a work of art, I think we have no other to compare with it in philosophic richness and perfection of execution, both in its grand design and its smallest detail. In a way, it is hard to think of it as having been written over many years. In spite of its epic proportions and encyclopaedic character, its astonishing union of massive erudition and poetic splendour and variety, the poem is so minutely articulated that it gives the impression of being a kind of natural phenomenon, or of having existed all at once in the poet's imagination.

We have only to think of Dante's inexhaustible ingenuity in calling attention time after time in different ways to his own solidity amidst the surrounding spirits; or the extraordinary way in which the laborious movements of the characters at the beginning of Purgatory become gradually lighter and easier as they are slowly freed from the weight of sin; or, how the prophetic moments which mark the rhythms of the pilgrim's gradually expanding consciousness change their modes, from the obscurity of the prophecies in Hell, where vision is indeed through a glass darkly, to the progressively clearer prophecies of Purgatory and Paradise which, like those of the greatest of the prophets of Israel, herald unequivocally the judgment of God on human evil.

The *Commedia* is also a love poem constructed according to a definition of love so encompassing that Dante is able to preserve all of the fruits of his experience—intellectual and moral, particular and universal, private and public—in terms of a journey whose propelling force is finally revealed as the love which moves the sun and other stars. Love, in this poem, is the principle which establishes order and also the principle through which men transcend any finite vision of order, for love both creates order and mediates the passage through successive degrees of it.

The personal focus for the theme of love is, of course, the love of Dante for Beatrice. It is no ordinary love but a "love-death," for Beatrice gained in beauty and value in her death, became in dying, more, not less, worthy of Dante's love. Her death, in spite of Dante's period of error in which he turned from her, served finally to lure his love in the direction of the God in whose presence Beatrice went to dwell eternally. She has been a puzzle to some interpreters of the poem because they have failed to grasp that she occupied a distinct and unique role in his life, a role different from that held by any other woman. She was not merely a "thing," so to speak, a reality, but a sign as well, a vehicle of God's grace and a metaphor for the divine. She never contained ambiguously all, or even most, of the various possibilities potential in the relationship between men and women. In her, as nowhere else, he discovered infinite value, and in the pursuit of her beauty found truth.

Dante's great poem is the most complete ordering of moral experience we possess because it is such a love poem, and because each man's final definition is created by the history of what he has loved and how he has loved it, and what he has failed to love. Love, the ordering principle, is therefore also the principle by which Dante, the questing pilgrim of the poem, achieves ideal self-definition, for all that he learns and all the changes that occur in his will and his mind rest on a gradual ordering of his desire. Each physical level of the poem represents a state of desire, one that Dante must know about in order to shun, or one which he must conform to, and the language and action of each level define that state. Since knowledge, too, is a function of the state of desire, what we know at any level of the poem concerning the order of things corresponds only to what is available to the pilgrim at that particular stage in his journey. The architectural structure of the poem, the order created by the hierarchy of love, demands that the same themes—the nature of love, the creative activity of God—be reintroduced at different levels of the journey in more complete and profound ways *pari passu* with the growth of the pilgrim's power to understand.

Dante enters the dark wood as a sinner, one who lives in a system of self which is encapsulated, closed, distorted, a self so structured that it can do nothing other than perpetuate its own burdensome identity. The pilgrim's state is one of despair, a state of will which reduplicates its misery in the very attempt to escape it. At such a moment Everyman must wait on grace. If he is to reach the goal of his journey there must be mediation, something must come from the "outside" to break the circle of self. The term "outside" is, of course, a spatial metaphor applied to an event whose true locus is consciousness, an event which may be understood as an absolutely primary and mysterious alteration of the self to make the journey at all possible. Dante's tremendous effort to escape the circle of self begins to succeed with the apparently mysterious and unforeseen advent of Virgil. The effort succeeds and yet does not succeed, for effort, however great, is not enough: "I yet not I." Virgil comes at the behest of Beatrice in a chain of grace descending from the Virgin through St. Lucy, the three ladies in heaven who break the vicious circularity of the fallen will and make it possible for Dante to relinquish the rhythms of despair for those of the expansion of consciousness. Had all these mediators not existed Dante would have remained at the foot of the delectable mountain, like that anguished pilgrim in Kafka's *Castle*. One must somehow be teachable in order to be taught, movable in order to be moved, savable in order to be saved. Possibilities of this sort cannot be coercively actualized. Their realization in any individual instance is as unintelligible as those particulars Plato relegated to a semi-illusory realm of being.

Dante's metaphor of the journey through the three realms of the beyond—it is of course a poem about this life as diffracted through a next world—enables him to give a final definition to different states of the will, to different qualities of desire. No one of his realms of eternity is quite like this life and, therefore, each one of them can comment on our existence. The community of Hell is one where men live in desire but without hope, the pilgrims in Purgatory know what they should wish and are certain in the hope of realizing their

desire—a relation between hope and wish certainly not of this world—
and the blessed in Paradise have a mode of existence in which desire
is fulfilled before it states itself and hope is realized the instant it is
generated. As "unwordly" as these states may be, the poetic texture
in which they are represented is intensely this-worldly. Through metaphor, symbol, historical and biographical allusion, through the vivid
memories of all the spirits who reveal themselves to him, Dante pours
the whole of this world into the next. Thus the departed are not
inhabitants of another world, but the inhabitants of this world, eternalized, defined, detached from the ambiguities of temporal existence,
and raised to a higher power.

I have said that Dante orders moral experience, but I should add
that he does so without simplifying it. The very Hell of his imagination is an infinitely more differentiated and graded place than the
Hell of the theologians, and his Purgatory is filled with light, learning,
and courtesy. This of course is obvious, but one remarkably obtuse
reading of the *Divina Commedia* concludes that Dante puts his
enemies in Hell and his friends in Purgatory or Paradise. Such readers
identify the meaning of the poem with its surface structure, with that
moral system in which all the characters find their respective places,
and identify the poet with the latter. If Dante everywhere immediately
condemned where his God condemned or everywhere saved where his
God saved, if he everywhere judged as his God judged, then the
Divina Commedia would have been some sort of literary curiosity. But
sometimes the judgment of his God weighs as heavily upon Dante
as it does on the damned, he is as puzzled as we are at the workings
of a divine will which saves Ripheus but leaves Virgil in Limbo. We
frequently find a tension between the judgment of a fallible human
pilgrim—still in the process of being matured by the flame of love
without which fire whole ranges of knowledge evade understanding—
and the judgment of his guide or the implicit judgment of God.
Sometimes these perspectives intersect in different ways without
wholly absorbing each other and, at other times, they would appear
effortlessly to coincide. Dante faints with pity at the destiny of Paolo
and Francesca, but enjoys Virgil's approval when he expresses con-
tempt for the wrathful Filippo Argenti. In fact, the pilgrim can even
compound the cruelty of the infernal system. No reader can forget
how, deep in the frozen bottom of Hell, Dante breaks his word to

Fra Alberigo, refusing to ease his pain by removing the ice from his eyes after having promised to do so, explaining that churlishness was, in this case, true courtesy. Here we are far from that tragic sense of the disproportion between guilt and retribution which we feel in some of the most poignant episodes of the *Inferno*. Indeed, we are shocked by the pilgrim's vindictiveness.

But courtesy, the proper action in any circumstance, should not fully contravene true morality, and the moral co-ordinates of any episode in the *Divina Commedia* are finally those of Dante's God, however the pilgrim may react and however savage or incomprehensible the destiny of the dead. What gives the poem its moral richness and its complexity is not this final, sometimes incomprehensible transcendental judgment, but the interplay between the reactions of the pilgrim and the views of his mediators as they reflect on the experiences they confront. It is precisely the elements of irrationality and savagery in Dante's moral universe which permit him to take account of the dark complexities of the one life we really have. For much of his journey, Dante is ignorant of many things and prone to misplace both his pity and his assent. He must learn to bend his will to the divine will, and the locus of moral and literary value for us resides in the variousness of his reactions to this absolute demand. The poem, as a poem, cannot demand our assent or coerce our consciences. It does what great literature must do and specifies the texture of experience. Dante's propositions and beliefs are often hopelessly irrelevant to us. But they served to guide the poet's mind and eye, and focus them on what the real world in all its variousness is like. Dante, like Shakespeare, finally captures for us, from that variousness, some of the many ways in which men may dispose of that finite quantum of energy they bring into the world.

The *Divina Commedia* is, in an obvious if not a strict use of the term, a drama. It has many great scenes which represent action or reveal character as action, and we move from one to another of them through a continually varying landscape. Indeed, the *Commedia* has more action and less narrative than any poem of similar dimensions. But the visible drama, so to speak, is contained within the greater drama of Dante's self, the dramatic relations between the objectified "lower" self of the pilgrim, Dante as the learner undertaking the journey, and Dante the poet who knows everything that the pilgrim must learn. These two selves, at the beginning of the poem, are far apart, and gradually converge until they are one at the end. In a sense it would be true to say that one of the themes of the poem is that of a man catching up with his final definition of self, if we take the standpoint of the poet, or of a man seeking final definition, if we take the standpoint of the pilgrim.

These two aspects of the self presented in the poem sometimes confront each other in marvellously complex ways. Thus, on the Ledge of Pride in Purgatory, when the *pilgrim* assumes the stooped position of the penitents and talks to Oderisi, the great illuminator of manuscripts, the *poet* has Oderisi speak of the transience of artistic fame and makes him refer to the advent of another poet who will eclipse the two Guido's, Guinizelli and Cavalcante. This new poet is obviously Dante himself, so the poet commits the sin of pride at the very moment the pilgrim is beginning its purgation. The situation is marvellously right, for it is of the essence of pride to reveal itself in the desire to remove it. It is insistently present until it is utterly gone.

The drama of self-confrontation is part of the greater drama of Dante's consciousness as it meets true reality in all of its strangeness, for Dante's God has the structure of what any man must call reality, whatever his beliefs. Its ways are not our ways, its "justice" not our "justice" and we must yield, however reluctantly at some points and however joyously at others, to an order we did not create but which, rather, created us. Dante's world is an other-worldly paradigm of this one precisely because it comprehends really irretrievable losses and because we are what we have somehow chosen to be, whatever blindness and compulsion may have dominated the will. In a sense, the inhabitants of Dante's Hell are not in the hands of an angry God but in their own. Dante's world is one in which the final vision of things and the human perception of these same things are contiguous only at some points, and the task of the pilgrim is that of rising to that other vision that is possessed by the poet. Thus Dante can comprehend all the beauty, pathos, and poignancy of the fate of the noble pagans of antiquity but nevertheless leave them in the Hell he found them in.

How difficult this was for him we can grasp when we recall how frequently and abundantly he expressed his love for the ancient world. He loved the Romans as few men of his time could, so much so that the *Divina Commedia* is incessantly drawing parallels and making analogies with the great events and figures of Roman history. Classical and Christian analogies are worked out in great detail throughout the poem and sometimes the juxtapositions are original and startling. Thus Dante takes the traditional typological parallel between Moses and St. Paul and replaces it by a parallel between Aeneas and St. Paul. It is then a pagan, doomed to Limbo, who nevertheless prefigures the great Apostle, for both made great journeys to the beyond to prepare themselves for parallel missions in this world, the one creating a universal Empire, the other a universal Church.

Yet Dante must limit his acceptance of things Roman because that past was, in the final analysis, only a prefiguration of true reality, an adumbration of salvation without the latter's power. Virgil, to be sure, is the perfect embodiment of reason, so much so that he can get along better in Purgatory than Dante, in spite of the fact that he has never been there before. But we are never allowed to forget Virgil's consciousness of what he has lost, his nostalgia for a bliss he never tasted but which he now knows exists and which will lie forever beyond his reach. Virgil's elegiac mood is paralleled by the frequently elegiac and nostalgic character of Dante's feeling for both classical antiquity and for Virgil himself as the representative figure of all that was best in that world. And Dante's Virgil strikes us as truly representative of *Romanitas*, as the first great post-classical representation of Roman ideals which we can recognize as somehow truly historical, as the product of a singular act of both the poetical and the historical imagination.

The figure of Virgil expresses not only a re-creation of a past, but Dante's relation to that past. Dante's destiny will transcend the destiny of his master while comprehending it, just as the *Commedia*, in some sense, contains and surpasses the *Aeneid*. This greater destiny is possible because both poet and poem are Christian. Virgil can traverse the palpable, gross reality of the *Inferno*, and the luminous crystalline atmosphere of the *Purgatorio*, but is forever barred from the blinding splendors of the *Paradiso*. Each great realm of the beyond has its own visual properties and Virgil's vision can accommodate only two.

The qualitative differences in the landscapes are expressed in the different metaphorical textures of each realm, so that the metaphors of the *Inferno* are most often used for describing what things actually look like, the more frequently complex and subtle metaphors of the *Purgatorio* often subordinate visual to moral and intellectual definition. The *Paradiso* has about one-third more similes than the previous *cantiche*, and they serve both to increase our understanding and to enrich what would have remained a virtually undifferentiated brightness. We do not see more of heaven through them, but we see many of the things of this world serving as clues to what the states of consciousness in heaven might be like.

In one way, the poem is a gallery of modes of vision correlated to the ever expanding consciousness and awareness of the pilgrim. The poem's general trend towards increasing subtlety and intellectuality of metaphorical texture corresponds to the increasing complexity of the experiences those metaphors define. As the life of the pilgrim expands it becomes more difficult of definition and exhausts more and more of the poet's genius.

Within the diversity of poetic texture in the poem Dante comprehends, in a kind of virtuoso synthesis, many of the great poetic moments of the past, the high points in the history of the imagination, and even surpasses that past. His Earthly Paradise is a truer, final rendering of the classical poetic vision of a golden age, that vision of a reality which the pagan poets somehow comprehended even when the pagan philosophers could not, thereby exceeding the powers of reason through their sacred gift of imagination. In the *Inferno*, Dante gives us a set of double metamorphoses which surpass the single ones of Ovid and Lucan. Pier delle Vigne, in the Wood of the Suicides, speaks in the accents of his own poetic idiom, and Arnaut Daniel speaks in his very own Provençal tongue. In this sense, therefore, the *Commedia* completes and extends the poetic possibilities of the past. As Dante surpasses Virgil through grace, he surpasses his immediate Italian predecessors through being the kind of poet who writes what love dictates. He surpasses the past, however, not by annihilating it, but by incorporating and transcending it.

Inferno

Dante begins his journey and enters Hell at the very watershed of his life, at the ideal age of thirty-five. The cosmic setting corresponds to no actual time. It is unique and charged with meaning, for the year is 1300, the season Spring, the day is the eve of Good Friday, and the great cosmic clock of spheres, stars, and planets has assumed the setting it had at the creation. Every measure of time and space points to the great drama of salvation, to the mystery of the origin of the universe and man, and the mystery of man's Fall and Redemption. The temporal and spatial co-ordinates of the journey will always be given to us by the great cosmic clock, fully visible and constantly present only in Purgatory, for Hell blocks it from view, and in Heaven we are within it.

The idea of Hell has frequently been a vehicle for the sadistic fantasies of "nice" people, fond of imagining a vengeful divinity implacably torturing other people they think belong there. Berdyaev said flatly that it was the invention of the "good," and the sharp intellect of Nietzsche saw that, if the inscription over the gate of Dante's Hell declares it the creation of love, an inscription to be placed over his Paradise might well read that Heaven was created by hate. Nietzsche doubtless had in mind the theological proposition held by St. Thomas and others that the bliss of the saved was perfected by their knowledge of the sufferings of the damned, a doctrine which Dante doubtless knew but avoided using out of poetic if not moral tact.

From the imaginative point of view Dante had little more than such propositions and the crude delusions of popular fantasy to begin with. Research into analogues and possible sources of Dante's *Inferno* simply serves to demonstrate how immeasurably superior Dante was, both imaginatively and morally, to his predecessors. With little help from tradition, learned and popular, he constructed a rich and ordered moral realm as superior to the crudities of that tradition as the Greek tragedies are to the raw and bloody stories which were their prehistoric origins. Like the tragedians of Greece, Dante is not only a great interpreter of myth but a maker of them. His Hell is truly a moral category because its inhabitants are not sent there by anything external to them, but because Hell is what they really wanted. Whatever Dante as a man may have believed as to the objective reality of Hell, his poetic tact creates a Hell which is intelligible and by which we can expand our moral awareness because it tells us about ourselves here and now. All of the damned chose something less than the finite and they get in return the finite eternalized. In other words they are stuck with themselves for all time, confined to the circle of self by a final definition which compels them to repeat their sins and perpetuate their identities forever.

Of course, there is a sense in which every one of the conditions in Hell, seen from the point of view of actual life, is remediable, but the poem views all of the human condition from the standpoint of death, from the standpoint of a final definition, and such a standpoint, if it is to be faithful to reality as honest men have known it to be, must imply that some things are really final. We might also consider the temporal infinity of Dante's other world as a metaphor for a qualitative infinity. Hell and Heaven, for example, may be understood as inhabited by people who have entered into states of despair or of bliss which are perpetually self-duplicating, because of either a vicious or a virtuous circularity of the will.

The infernal character which finite values and goods come to possess when protracted to infinity applies to many laudable activities and values. Hell, therefore, is a place not only for obviously evil men. We find there men of considerable virtue. Aristotle and other noble pagans, for example, are in Limbo, where they are, to be sure, spared overt punishment. Dante's theology compelled him to put them there, however reluctantly. But he does something more than merely follow a theological formula blindly. The great men of pagan antiquity are at the same level of existence as those unbaptized infants who share Limbo with them, the uncomprehending witnesses of an endless seminar, of an eternal melancholy colloquium among the very princes of humanism. The point of all this is not finally a dogmatic one but a moral and human one: if there are some truths which it is indispensable for a man to know, and he doesn't know them, then no matter how much else he does know he might just as well know nothing. Other great universes of value besides humanism are again admired, imagined, judged, and condemned: in the Paolo and Francesca episode, the world of romantic love with all its grace, beauty, chivalry, and poignancy, and in the Ulysses episode, the world of Faustian love for universal experience, with its portrayal of the heroic thirst for an unlimited and immediate knowledge of life. In these cases as elsewhere in the poem Dante gives us what Yeats saw as the essence of great poetry: "Character isolated by a deed / To engross the present and dominate memory."

Purgatorio

Dante enters Purgatory as a man seeking salvation and as an artist seeking definition. He can achieve both of these goals—they are finally one—because the imagination is at the root of both charity and poetry. It is the faculty by which you recognize who is your neighbour and it is the faculty which breaks the bonds of habit and reveals the uncommonness of what is common. The pilgrim here learns to love through many confrontations which are also self-confrontations. He considers his art through many conversations with artists—an artistic community contained within that larger community of saints the boundaries of which are not confined by space or time—he learns the sources of his talent and is constrained to reflect on the complex and paradoxical relations which obtain between a man's destiny as a man and a man's destiny as an artist, or between the destinies of the public and the private self.

This last theme, which runs through the whole of the *Divina Commedia*, reaches its climax in the *Purgatorio* with the encounter of Virgil and Statius. Virgil, like all true poets, possesses divine gifts. Moreover, his work and examples are among the most important reasons for Statius' achievement as an artist, a far lesser one than Virgil's own. But Virgil, in Dante's drama, was also, through his "Messianic" Fourth Eclogue, misread for centuries as a prophecy of the coming of Christianity, the unconscious instrument of Statius' salvation even though he is himself doomed to Limbo. Nowhere else in the poem does Virgil's recurrent awareness of his loss strike us with more poignancy, nowhere else is he more filled with a patient and gracious endurance of his privation, and nowhere else does the warm human love which binds the three poets make divine judgment seem more unjust.

Artistic achievement, Dante tells us—and it was a lesson he had to learn—it not necessarily a means of grace for the possessor of artistic gifts, however paradoxically his life and work may have channelled grace to others. Our final destiny resides deep in the privacy of the self and is incommensurable with whatever public or historical self we may bequeath to the world. Virgil is a tragic instance of the truly great teacher in the ancient tradition of the esoteric guide. He gives his student everything he has to give, as his companion through experience, and then relinquishes him, leaving him to follow out his destiny however different from his own. In a way, Virgil is the most charitable figure in the whole of the *Divina Commedia*, for he gives to others a preparatory knowledge and wisdom which cannot do for him what it can do for those others. The possessor of virtue and knowledge in the highest humanly possible degree, he knows that they are not enough for salvation, knows that salvation cannot be coerced or earned, yet can give all that is in him to give.

Dante prepares to leave Purgatory by drinking, in the Earthly Paradise, of the streams Lethe and Eunoë, the waters of one purging the memory of sin, the waters of the other restoring a transformed memory of all things. By this point in the journey Virgil has completed his task. Dante's will is upright, and he has been crowned and mitred over himself, that is to say he no longer stands in needs of the corrective and guiding powers of Empire and Church. This would seem to be enough preparation for the paradisiacal journey. But Dante is telling us that the restoration of human nature requires more than the rectification of the will and the ordering of love. It requires the reconstruction of the memory, a perfect detachment from the moral weight of the past. The journey through Hell and Purgatory had all been a preparation for this possibility. Lethe makes Dante forget all his sins and errors, but this amnesia is temporary, for a self ready for Paradise cannot deny what it has been by permanently forgetting what it would not like to remember. Eunoë restores the memory, but so restructured that the evils of the past are transcended and no longer reach into the present. Man must not only accept forgiveness but must also be freed from repentance and remorse.

In *Paradiso* IX, where Dante encounters the great troubadour Folco in the heaven of Venus, one of those heavens in the earth's shadow as a sign of the remote touch of earthiness that still somehow touches their splendour, we learn that the blessed see all things in God. Folco remembers his amorous past but the fault of it does not enter his mind. Repentance has been transmuted into praise of God. He can look upon his past and smile in joy at the divine power which ordained and foresaw, admire the art which adorns the great outcome of all things with beauty. Dante too will come to see all things, good and evil, personal and universal, his sins and his good actions, as they exist in the mind of God, under the aspect of eternity. Freed from guilt and fear, from *bondage* to the past and to experience, he will see that all things somehow had to be the way they were. The recovery of Eden, therefore, is not the recovery of a *tabula rasa*, a reversion to childish innocence. It is a higher synthesis of innocence and experience, a state in which memory of experience has lost its power to oppress and recovered innocence does not obliterate knowledge.

At the centre of the *Purgatorio*, at the very heart of the poem, is a sequence of cantos on love, the longest continuous exposition of love in the poem. Dante has now learned enough and—more important—changed enough, to comprehend what his guide will teach him. He is ripening in the flame of love, and everywhere in the *Purgatorio* he has been met with an increasingly exquisite courtesy, a courtesy which is gradually ripening into charity. Hell had its courtesy too, a courtesy of which it is true to say that to be courteous may be to be discourteous. But in Purgatory we are not in a community unified and blinded by hate, and continually on the verge of egoistic fragmentation. Whereas the damned so often demanded fame of the pilgrim, demanded to be remembered even in their degraded identities, the souls in Purgatory ask for prayers to speed their journey. Dante is now in a true community, for not only do the souls need his prayers but he needs their instruction, and all possess the inner disposition which manners require if they are to be fulfilled in love.

Their freedom from hate enables them to see even when their punishments blind them physically, at those times when spiritual vision must be trained at the expense of physical vision. The stitched eyes of the envious which force them to lean on one another for aid remind them that they looked at others wrongly. They know now that envy is a denial of mutuality. The smoke which blinds the angry and compels them to move by hearing alone suggests that the angry do not really see at all, even in a distorted way. The sufferings of the penitents in Purgatory, unlike those of the damned, serve to increase their vision and therefore their love and knowledge. Their journey up the mountain is marked by the great moments of the liturgy of the Church which are now no longer ritual but actuality. Where earthly ritual repeats itself, purgatorial ritual serves to celebrate once for all each stage in the progressive disburdening of self from the weight of sin.

The purgatorial state is marked by Dante's constant participation in the life of this realm of the beyond. He ceases to be a spectator, and his discourse with the penitents is marked by engagement. The pilgrim and penitents petition each other's aid with exquisite tact, and refer to themselves or each other with great insight and delicacy. One example among the many in Purgatory of the subtlety and character of this new sense of human relationship is the marvellous brief encounter with La Pia in the fifth canto. She waits in Ante-Purgatory with others who repented at the last hour. We know how much she must desire entry into active purgation, yet she defines herself to Dante with quietness and brevity, and modestly asks for his prayers. Mindful of the fact that he may well be tired after his tremendous journey she remembers he may need to rest a while before he prays for her, and courteously inserts a brief injunction in her seven-line utterance.

> "Deh, quando tu sarai tornato al mondo,
>   e riposato della lunga via,"
>   seguitò il terzo spirito al seconda
>
> "ricorditi di me che son la Pia:
>   Siena mi fè; disfecemi Maremma:
>   salsi colui che'nnanellata pria
>
> disposando m'avea con la sua gemma." (*Pug.* V, 130–136)

The courtesy of the *Purgatorio* is a function of love, imperfect as yet, but a love certain to become charity, that charity which in Paradise will be so great that the souls delight in talking to Dante even though they already know all that he will say and do, and even though they have no need of any assistance from him.

We are told of the source of this love which has been revealing itself as courtesy in Marco Lombardo's explanation in *Purgatorio* XVI. Marco explains that in the moment when God created the individual soul, it enjoyed a prenatal instant of beatific vision. When the child is born, it cannot remember the content or substance of this vision, but recalls it only in the obscure form of its own experience of its restless desire. Unable to truly remember, the embodied soul is compelled to repeat. It is compelled to seek repetitively and fruitlessly for the unknown object of its desire. The goal of desire is known, in this state of amnesia, only by negation, by the fact that all available pleasures, all finite pleasures, are disappointing. As Dante tells us in the *Convivio*, the child reaches out first after an apple, then as it grows older it wants a horse, and then a woman, then money and still more money, always seeking and always dissatisfied. The final, indeed, the only task of Church and Empire, the two universal ordering institutions, is to guide this love in the proper direction.

Love then rests on memory, and the guidance of love depends on the conquest of forgetfulness, for love is nostalgia for a bliss from which existence has separated us, the kind of nostalgia the mystic feels, as Dante tells us at the close of the *Comedy*, when having returned from his vision of the Absolute he cannot recall the substance of his vision but is like one who, having wakened from a dream, feels its bliss, its "imprinted passion," without being able to recapture its substance. Or, in another image the poet uses, he is like the visionary who tries to remember for us what he saw and checks the small quantity of truth he can wrest from memory against the sweetness which distils itself from his heart whenever he captures true images from the abyss of memory. For memory is inexhaustible, and the contents of memory can only be permanently and fully actualized in the beatific vision. At the bottom of the abyss of memory lies the vision of God, and the Hell in the memory is finally only a stage in that inward journey. The reconstruction of memory and the exploration of memory are finally to be understood as two aspects of the single process of redemption.

Paradiso

While the *Inferno* and the *Purgatorio*, in their respective ways, are concerned with the correction of moral error, the *Paradiso*, as a journey through the intelligible universe, celebrates truth and involves primarily the correction of the pilgrim's intellectual error. The *Paradiso* is philosophical poetry in the obvious meaning of the term in that it is passionately involved with ideas, but it is also philosophical poetry in a more precise sense: it renders a systematically ordered world of pure thought in terms of images and events. The ideas, indeed, are the poetry, and do not stand outside of it. Dante, like Shakespeare, is one of the supreme poets who can say anything, no matter how vulgar or how intellectual, and make it artistically right. We may recall the story of St. Francis and his marriage to Lady Poverty in *Paradiso* XI where Dante can unite in one imaginative representation power and humility, beauty and ugliness, repugnance and attraction, demonstrating a capacity to assimilate disparate things which we would find impossible. And there is in his heterogeneous couplings no sense of the strain that we often feel in a Donne or a Crashaw who, at times, seem to be preserving by force an imaginative possibility which was somehow natural to Dante.

To the extent that the *Inferno* and *Purgatorio* primarily deal with virtue, they bear on the ethical realm and are dramatic and psychological. Readers of the *Paradiso* are sometimes disappointed because it lacks those dramatic qualities which dominate the previous *cantiche* and which, we generally assume, are central to literature. For Dante, however, the ethical realm and the life of moral conflict and choice prepare the way for a life of ideal emotional and intellectual activities. The ultimate objects of desire are not actions but states of mind and spirit—love, joy, understanding. The *Paradiso* evokes a "life beyond life," pure spontaneity which transcends morality and the ordinary forms of human experience. Hence its lyrical and evocative character, the subjective mode in which Dante describes this part of the universe. He is, in a way, the single character in this part of the poem, the only one still capable of surprise. What we feel about his experience at this stage of the journey we feel through the effect his various experiences have on him.

Throughout the *Paradiso* the great drama is played through the eyes of Dante as they seek light and find beauty, first in the eyes of another, then everywhere. Each moment of ascent from sphere to sphere is a rapture in which Dante looks into the eyes of Beatrice: she grows in luminosity, he grows in love, and passes into an ecstasy from which he wakes to find himself on a higher plane of reality and truth. Thus the ascent through the spheres is a circularity of power, a *virtuous* circularity: increase of light and beauty is followed by an increase of love and knowledge, which in turn demands more love, and so from sphere to sphere. The first twenty-nine cantos of the *Paradiso* take place in space and time, and we learn early that the souls whom Dante meets manifest themselves to him in the spheres in accommodation to his limitations of vision, having their true abode in the Empyrean.

The spheres are, indeed, screens, in which the souls project themselves, making of themselves accommodative metaphors of their own higher mode of being, a mode which Dante's vision will gradually become strong enough to apprehend. The climactic moment for the theme of the increase of Dante's power of vision comes in Canto XXX, in which Dante describes his acquisition of a new power of sight, a *novella vista*, a power of vision which has all the immediacy of physical sight but whose object is that of thought, a faculty which is a synthesis of thought and sense with both functions raised to a higher power.

Throughout the final cantos of the poem Dante repeats some form of the verb "to see" or the noun "light" with such insistence that the effect would have been absurd were he not signifying the divine. The simplest of rhetorical devices, repetition, is here miraculously adequate to the most unimaginable of experiences, the simultaneous and direct vision of heaven and God finally reached after the many serial and progressive approximations the pilgrim has traversed in the journey to his goal.

As Dante begins to acquire his *novella vista* Beatrice explains that the first visions he sees are only adumbrations or metaphors of the reality he seeks and which he will grasp as it really is when his new-found faculty strengthens itself. *Paradiso* XXX (28 ff.) thus begins a rapidly transforming sequence of images and visions, of metaphors, which are all theophanies, each one a closer approximation of ultimate reality. Here Dante reveals himself a master of the poetry of metamorphosis, and makes a use of metamorphosis unlike any poet either before or after him. The *Metamorphoses* of Ovid finally point to the unity of all things in the great transforming flux of nature. Dante's own weird metamorphoses in the *Inferno*, the reciprocal transformations of reptiles and men, were in the service of the imaginative representation of that loss of identity implied by a thievish will which cannot distinguish between what is one's own and what belongs to another. Now Dante will place the metamorphosis of imagery in the service of expanding vision.

And vision expands with an unexpected result. Paradise, which for so many cantos was always about to dissolve into ecstasy, is suddenly gathered into absolute concreteness. For a long time we saw only soul-lights manifesting themselves, first singly, then in pairs, and then in patterns of ever growing complexity. We saw these points of light frequently described in terms of the dance or of other symbols of harmony and of the integration of multiplicity within unity. Visually speaking, the souls were seen in an impersonal mode. But now the angels and spirits become individual and palpable again, and the final vision of God will not disappear into blankness but will comprehend the Incarnation, the revelation of divinity through a human personality in its highest mode of being and action.

The final canto of the poem begins with a beautiful prayer addressed on Dante's behalf by St. Bernard to the Virgin. Dante is no longer the poet, the thinker, the moralist, but a simple devout soul. The ultimate in grace is given, if at all, only to prayer, and it is at St. Bernard's behest that the divine essence unfolds itself to Dante, first as the God of the philosophers, One, True, Good, then as the God of Christian revelation, Triune and Incarnate.

The divine has been approached through poetic veils and masks, progressive symbols, until, in a sense, language is gone and replaced by vision. The whole journey now seems to have been nothing more than a series of theophanies expressed in symbol and event which served to guide us to the final moment of direct apprehension. Dante has gradually reduced what are objects of thought—the discourse of philosophers and theologians—to objects of sight. The ultimate sight, in a way, lies outside the poem, for it is what Dante sees when he relinquishes the fallible, rectilinear motion of time for the uniform motion of eternity, the motion he adopts in the last lines when his will is completely one with the love that moves the sun and other stars. Thus the poem ends in silence and vision. The end is as implicitly rich as it is because, through Dante's poetic genius, it has been somehow made to include all that we have been through to get there with him. Dante's metaphors have taken us to the same goal which is the true end of the philosopher's quest and the saint's progress, for his images have not been decoration for philosophical abstractions but translucent vehicles of his intuition of truth.

Dante's Katabasis and Mission[*]

GIAN ROBERTO SAROLLI

DANTE'S CREATIVE TASK has been defined as of "superhuman difficulty." This is clearly discernible in the language of the poem; for although the *Commedia*, considered as a whole, seems astonishingly light and simple—thanks to its clear and orderly structure—there is no single passage that does not reflect tension and effort; one is left with the impression that the work at every step demanded of Dante a boundless devotion, an unstinting expenditure of himself. No less devotion, no less unstinting expenditure of self is demanded of Dante scholars when they are faced by the difficult question of whether or not it is prophetic.

Bruno Nardi, following in the footsteps of Pietrobono and Barbi, has stressed that:

Come Dante considera l'andata d'Enea ad "immortale secolo" concessa da Dio per singolare privilegio all'eroe troiano, al pari del ratto di Paolo "sive in corpore nescio, sive extra corpus nescio, Deus scit", così egli ritiene la visione profetica a sè concessa una grazia speciale di Dio che lo ha scelto a denunciara la "cagion che'l mondo ha fatto reo", e i disegni divini per il rinverdimento della pianta edenica, dispogliata per la seconda volta.[1]

The opposite theory is adhered to by Alessandro Passerin d'Entrèves who repeats the opinion of the great historian James Bryce that the *Monarchia* (and consequently the *Divina Commedia*) must be con-

---

[*]This study should be considered a new chapter of my earlier study: "Dante: 'scriba Dei'," in *Convivium* n.s. VI (1963), 385–422; 513–544; 641–671. For this reason, I am taking the liberty of referring the reader to the above work in order to avoid unneccessary bibliographical references and repetitions.

[1]B. Nardi, *Dante e la cultura medievale, nuovi saggi di filosofia dantesca* (Bari, 1942), 123–124.

sidered the epitaph of the Holy Roman Empire rather than a prophecy. Passerin d'Entrèves,[2] aware of what we might call the Hamletic doubt in Dante studies, points out further that the "'glorious dream of Dante' [Gentile] has been hailed as a prophecy or described as a mirage."

An idea similar to that of Bryce is expressed, *mutatis mutandis*, in Ernest Curtius' classic *European Literature and the Latin Middle Ages*.[3] The renowned German scholar pointed out that the central message of the *Divina Commedia* can be grasped when it is recognized that Beatrice as well as the three beasts defeated by the Veltro and the DXV represent a theological system transformed into a prophetic one. Curtius states that this message

concerns a prophecy whose fulfilment he [Dante] expected in the immediate future. When he died at 56, his certainty was presumably still unshaken. Had he reached the "perfect" age of 81 (*Conv.* IV xxiv, 6), he would perhaps have been obliged to admit the collapse of his historical construction. But he could not retract his work. His imperious spirit believed that it could command even the future. A future, however, which could envisage only fourteenth-century Italy. . . . Even if we could interpret his prophecy, that would give it no meaning for us. What Dante hid, Dante scholarship need not now unriddle. But it must take seriously the fact that Dante believed that he had an apocalyptic mission.[4]

Although the arduous task of solving the enigmas and difficult lines of Dante's work has met with the disapproval and mockery of almost all the critics, I believe that it is essential for the general interpretation of the *Divina Commedia* and of Dante's life. As an illustration, let me refer to my suggestion that the hidden meaning of both the Veltro and the DXV lies in a well-known christological symbol applicable, in terms of political theology, to Christ himself as well as to the Emperor as a *typus-Christi*, in accordance with the view of Kantorowicz.[5] Thus, Curtius' presentation of the problem, and the solution of the famous enigma enable us to arrive at the central message of the *Divina Commedia* and the very core of Dante's hope and mission. It is my opinion,

[2]A. Passerin d'Entrèves, *Dante as a Political Thinker* (Oxford, 1952), 2.

[3]E. Curtius, *European Literature and the Latin Middle Ages*, trans. Willard R. Trask (New York–Evanston, 1963). This English translation in the Bollingen series contains a final important appendix, "The Medieval Basis of Western Thought," added by the author to this translation only.

[4]*Ibid.*, 377.

[5]E. Kantorowicz, *The King's Two Bodies: A Study in Medieval Political Theology* (Princeton, 1957); see especially ch. 3, "Christ-centered Kingship," 42–86.

and Barbi's as well, that the whole structure of the *Divina Commedia* is based upon the prophetic urgency, and that, without the prophecy, the unsurpassed poem would achieve a less powerful immediacy of meaning. The above-mentioned political theology must be considered as an indispensable Ariadne guiding us through the apparent labyrinth of Dante's poetry. This can readily be understood if we consider the famous Canto XXV of the *Paradiso* in which the word *ritornerò*, significant because Dante never used words idly, reveals his twofold meaning, the double katabasis, the return to earth after his fateful journey, as St. Peter will say in *Paradiso* XXVII, 64–65: "E tu, figliuol, che per lo mortal pondo / *ancor giù tornerai*" (my italics)— before and/or after the exile to Florence, which is merely suggested in the *Paradiso* (XXV, 8–9): "*ritornerò poeta*; ed in sulfonte / del mio battesmo prenderò 'l cappello" (my italics)—and to God, *nunc* and *sub specie aeternitatis*.

Canto XXV of the *Paradiso* is well known but let us have before us its most significant passages:[6]

> Se mai continga che'l poema sacro
> al quale ha posto mano e cielo e terra,
> sì che m'ha fatto per più anni macro,
>
> vinca la crudeltà che fuor mi serra
> del bello ovile ov'io dormi'agnello,
> nimico ai lupi che li danno guerra,
>
> con altra voce omai, con altro vello
> ritornerò poeta; ed in sul fonte
> del mio battesmo prenderò'l cappello;
>
> però che ne la fede, che fa conte
> l'anime a Dio, quivi intra'io, e poi
> Pietro per lei sì mi girò la fronte.
>
> . . . .
>
> E quella pia che guidò le penne
> de le mie ali a così alto volo,
> a la risposta così mi prevenne:
>
> "La Chiesa militante alcun figliuolo
> non ha con più speranza, com'è scritto
> nel sol che raggia tutto nostro stuolo:

---

[6]All quotations of Dante are from *Le Opere di Dante, testo critico della Società Dantesca Italiana,* ed. M. Barbi *et al.* (2nd ed., Florence, 1960).

però li è conceduto che d'Egitto
vegna in Ierusalemme per vedere,
anzi che'l militar li sia prescritto."

. . . .

Ahi quanto ne la mente mi commossi,
quando mi volsi per veder Beatrice,
per non poter veder, ben che io fossi

presso di lei, e nel mondo felice!

(*Par.* XXV, 1–12; 49–57; 136–139)

There are many key words in these stanzas, but the most important
are *contingere* and *fede* in the first part, *speranza* and *militare* in the
second, and *vedere* both in the second part and at the end. Dante
scholars, misled by the opening conjunction "if" emphatically stressed
by the adverb "ever," have overlooked the significance of the verb
contingere, having always accepted its most banal meaning "to
happen," as a result of a *lectio facilior*. It will be sufficient to mention
Sapegno[7] as representing the Italian tradition, and Grandgent,[8] the
Anglo-American one. In addition, Niccolò Rodolico, in his *Lettura
Dantesca*,[9] states " 'Se mai'! le prime parole del canto rivelano l'incer-
tezza dell'effettuarsi della cosa sperata; è un sospiro nei regni di felicità
eterna; è un dubbio là proprio dove il dubbio non deve opprimere. È
il contrasto tra la speranza quale umanamente dubbiosa appare agli
uomini, e la speranza, certa di gloria."

Rodolico would probably have better understood this passage if he
had realized that Dante was using a typical example of *argumentatio
necessaria*, a rhetorical device codified by Cicero[10] and underlined by
Boethius[11] and by Marius Victorinus,[12] in order to focus our attention
on the following bare Latinism *contingere*; there is an obvious connection with St. Thomas Aquinas' distinction between *contingentia*
and *necessitas* (*Summa Theol.* I, Q. 22, A. 4; Q. 14, A. 13), or,

[7]*La Divina Commedia*, ed. N. Sapegno (Milan–Naples, 1957), *s.v.* "continga."
[8]*La Divina Commedia di Dante Alighieri*, ed. and annotated by C. H. Grandgent,
rev. ed. (Boston, 1933), *s.v.* "continga."
[9]N. Rodolico, "Il canto XXV del *Paradiso*," in *Letture Dantesche*, v. III, ed.
G. Getto (Florence, 1961), 134.
[10]*Opera rhetorica*; *De Inventione* II, xxix, par. 44, ed. Friedrich (Leipzig, 1893),
I, 145.
[11]*Commentaria in Topica Ciceronis: De differentiis topicis* III, in *Patrologia
Latina* 64, col. 1198.
[12]C. Halm, *Rhetores Latini Minores* (photostat) (Frankfurt/Main, 1964), 231–
236. For Victorinus in the eleventh and twelfth centuries, see J. de Ghellinck, S. J.,
Le mouvement théologique du XIIe siècle (2nd ed., Bruges, 1948), 289–296.

perhaps better, between *contingens* and *necessarius* in the *Summa Contra Gentiles* (I, 67). In the quoted passage the great soul of the poet is expressing in pure Christian terms not his *dubbio*, but what I would like to call his *theological humility*, which finds its counterpart in his stylistic and rhetorical humility, his careful choice, according to the *rota Virgili*,[13] of the very *humiles* (elegiac) words (and let us not forget that the messianic prophecy of Virgil is contained in the well-known *Eclogue*): *agnello* and *ovile*, for example, and *cappello* for laurel (or something else that I shall advance later on as my own hypothesis). His theological humility can be interpreted as a *certezza* provided that such a *certezza* was written in the great book of the Universe, in the Mind of God, the macrocosm corresponding perfectly to the microcosm[14] represented at one and the same time by Dante and the *Divina Commedia*. Of course one cannot deny that the verb *continga* at first glance appears to have no special connotation of fulfilment in Dante's passage; rather, it seems to reflect the poet's uncertainty in his hope. But it is used in this same Canto XXV when Dante is undergoing the examination in hope by St. James, and when Dante himself is defined by Beatrice as *speranza* of the Militant Church (vv. 51–53), and this is the only occasion it is used in the whole vernacular corpus of the poet. For all these reasons, one cannot accept the *lectio facilior* without first examining the historical development of the word, and the wide range of associations contained in it.

Contingere had many meanings during the classical and mediaeval period, and at least one of these meanings underwent considerable development at the hands of the scholastic philosophers, particularly St. Thomas Aquinas. As a transitive verb, *contingo* (*con + tango =*

---

[13]E. Faral, *Les arts poétiques du XIIe et du XIIIe siècle: Recherches et documents sur la technique littéraire du moyen âge* (Paris, 1962), 87. On this point, see also A. Schiaffini, *Lettura del 'De Vulgari Eloquentia'* (Rome, Ateneo, 1958–59), 290.

[14]"Students of the Middle Ages and the Renaissance are now fully aware of an extensive and complex theory of macrocosmic-microcosmic harmony that once gave vitally and profoundly symbolic value to all aspects of music." This occurs in an interesting and enlightening article by Earl R. Wasserman ("Pope's 'Ode for Musick'," in *ELH* 28 (1961), 164) which I shall quote again in relation to the myth of Orpheus. For the problem of harmony and music in Dante's *Divina Commedia* and the macrocosmic-microcosmic harmony, see the posthumous book of Leo Spitzer, *Classical and Christian Ideas of World Harmony*, ed. A. Granville Hatcher (Baltimore, 1963).

I touch; the *Catholicon*, for example, offers glosses, especially for
contactus[15]) most frequently meant to touch physically, sometimes in
a hostile fashion, or to touch with something, as in anointing. In a
more figurative sense it denoted "to arrive at," "to reach something,"
"to border on something," "to be concerned with," or "to belong to."
In this latter sense we find the words of the prodigal son, "da mihi
portionem substantiae quae me contingit" (Luke 15:22). *Contingere*
as "belong to" would appear to have some relation to Dante's use of
the term—"if ever it would belong, be appropriate to, the sacred poem
. . . to defeat cruelty"—except for the fact that Dante used the verb
intransitively, and a transitive meaning must be considered incom-
patible. *Contingere* was widely used as an intransitive verb during the
classical and mediaeval period, and it is from this usage that modern
Dante commentators derive their interpretation. Intransitively it was
synonymous with *obvenire, evenire, accidere, concedere,* and *compe-
tere,* all of which denote "to happen" or "to befall." Priscian and
Isidore of Seville agreed with these meanings, the latter commenting
"contingit eventu, obtingit sorte, accidit casu, evenit vel malo vel
bono."[16] Since either good or evil could follow indifferently after
contingere,[17] nothing new has been added to the established meaning
of the verb.

Perhaps Aristotle's works on logic provide the basic meaning that
ultimately influenced Dante. In his *De interpretatione* and the *Analytica priora* he discussed the nature and varieties of syllogisms, and
drew a distinction between the necessary and "the possible" (the
contingent). The expression "to be possible" may be used in two ways:

In one, it means to happen generally and fall short of necessity, e.g. man's
turning grey or growing or decaying, or generally what naturally belongs
to a thing. . . . In another sense the expression means the indefinite, which
can be both thus and not thus, e.g. an animal's walking or an earthquake's
taking place while it is walking, or generally what happens by chance:

---

[15]*s.v.* "contagium"; there is the following: ". . . a contingo . . . per contactus
unius totus grex corrumpitur" (Johannes de Genoa, *Catholicon,* Aldini 54 of the
Library of the University of Pavia).

[16]*De Proprietate Sermonum vel Rerum: A Study and Critical Edition of a Set of
Verbal Distinctions,* Myra L. Uhlfelder ("Papers and Monographs of the American
Academy in Rome," XV [Rome, 1954]), 25.

[17]*The New Latin Dictionary* (London, Cassell, 1959), which deals with the classical period only, states that good luck is more likely to follow than evil.

for none of these inclines by nature in the one way more than in the opposite.[18]

In the early Middle Ages, Boethius' commentaries on Aristotle closely paralleled the master's text; for Boethius, *contingentia* was applied to the future. In defining *contingens*, he paraphrased Aristotle:

Contingens autem secundum Aristotelicam sententiam est quodcunque aut casus fert, aut ex libero cujuslibet arbitrio et propria voluntate venit, aut facilitate naturae in utramque partem redire possibile est, ut fiat scilicet, et non fiat. . . . In his autem quae in futuro sunt, et contingentia sunt, et fieri potest aliquid, et non fieri.[19]

It is in the works of Aquinas that the idea of contingency is removed from the syllogism and placed within the realm of Divine Providence. It would not be surprising if Dante, in opening his canto of hope, chose a verb that would echo his hope in Providence. In the *Summa Contra Gentiles*, Aquinas distinguished the contingent from the necessary in a way that would have been quite intelligible to Aristotle. The contingent and the necessary differ according to their relationship to their cause. The necessary can only *be*, that is, it must follow from its cause. The contingent can either be or not be—it can happen or not happen.[20] In the *Summa Theologica* St. Thomas discussed whether God can know future contingent things: concluding that God does know these, he distinguished between the contingent in act now and the contingent respecting the future (from man's point of view). Man can know only the present contingent with certain knowledge. God's way of knowing is basically different. "And although contingent things become actual successively, nevertheless God knows contingent things not successively, as they are in their own being, as we do; but simultaneously." This is because his knowledge is

---

[18]*Analytica priora* I, 13, in *The Works of Aristotle* (Oxford, 1928), vol. I. See also *De Interpretatione*, ch. 12 and *Analytica priora* I, 14–22, for a discussion of the various syllogisms involving one or more contingent premises.

[19]*In librum Aristotelis de interpretatione commentaria majora* III, *Patrologia Latina* 64, col. 489. See also "De Futuris Contingentibus," col. 495–518; "De Enuntiationibus Modorum Possibilis, Contingentis, Impossibilis, et Necessarii," col. 580–602 in the *Interpretatio priorum Analyticorum Aristotelis*; "De contingenti non necessario," I, xii, *ibid.*, col. 651–652, and a lengthy discussion, closely paralleling Aristotle, of syllogisms containing contingent propositions, in I, xiii, xxi, cols. 653, 666.

[20]I, 67: "Contingens a necessario differt secundum quod unumquodque in sua causa est. Contingens enim sic in sua causa est, ut non esse ex ea possit et esse; necessarium autem ex sua causa non potest non esse."

eternal, and all things in time are present to him from eternity. God's knowledge is certain; man, who knows only the causes of contingent things, has only a conjectural knowledge of future contingents.[21]

Aquinas re-emphasized the role of Providence in Question 22, Article 4 of the *Summa Theologica*, which deals with whether Providence imposes any necessity on things foreseen. He asserted that necessity is imposed on some things, but not all. Everything aims toward divine goodness, which is an extrinsic end to all things; after this, "the principal good in things themselves is the perfection of the universe; which would not be, were not all grades of being found in things. Whence it pertains to divine providence to produce every grade of being." Divine Providence has prepared causes that follow infallibly and of necessity for some things, and contingent causes for others, "according to the nature of their proximate causes."[22] Effects follow from contingent things if they are not prevented in some way. God knows not only the causes and results of contingents, but also knows how contingent causes may be impeded.[23]

Placing contingent events under the care of Divine Providence puts Dante's words "Se mai continga" in a new light. If we accept Beatrice's judgment that "La Chiesa militante alcun figliuolo / non ha con più speranza, *com'è scritto / nel sol . . .*" (52–54; my italics), then we may

[21]*Summa Theol.* Ia, Iae, q. 14, a. 13: ". . . considerandum est quod contingens aliquod dupliciter potest considerari. Uno modo in seipso, secundum quod iam actu est. . . . Alio modo potest considerari contingens, ut est in sua causa. . . . Unde quicumque cognoscit effectum contingentem in causa sua tantum, non habet de eo nisi coniecturalem cognitionem. . . Et licet contingentia fiant in actu successive, non tamen Deus successive cognoscit contingentia, prout sunt in suo esse, sicut nos sed simul. Quia sua cognitio mensuratur aeternitate, sicut etiam suum esse: aeternitas autem, tota simul existens, ambit totum tempus. . . ." The English quotations are from the translation by the Fathers of the English Dominican Province (2nd ed., London, 1920).

[22]"Respondeo dicendum quod providentia divina quibusdam rebus necessitatem imponit: non autem omnibus, ut quidam crediderunt. Ad providentiam enim pertinet ordinare res in finem. Post bonitatem autem divinam, quae est finis a rebus separatus, principale bonum in ipsis rebus existens, est perfectio universi: quae quidem non esset, si non omnes gradus essendi invenirentur in rebus. Unde ad divinam providentiam pertinet omnes gradus entium producere. Et ideo quibusdam effectibus praeparavit causas necessarias, ut necessario evenirent; quibusdam vero causas contingentes, ut evenirent contingenter, secundum conditionem proximarum causarum."

[23]"Amplius, sicut ex causa necessaria sequitur effectus certitudinaliter, ita ex causa contingenti completa, si non impediatur. Sed quum Deus cognoscat omnia . . . scit non solum causas contingentium, sed etiam ea quibus possunt impediri. Scit igitur per certitudinem an contingentia sint vel non sint." (*Summa Contra Gentiles* I, 67).

make the barest suggestion that Dante was indeed rich in the virtue of Hope, and would have been optimistic rather than pessimistic about the fate of his poem, his *milizia letteraria*, as I have elsewhere pointed out,[24] as well as of his mission. The fact that *continga*, *qua* verb, is a *hapaxlegomenon* in the *Divina Commedia*, and especially in this very peculiar passage, may well indicate that the poet intended it to have a very extraordinary meaning applicable here alone: "If it should fulfil the design of Divine Providence that the sacred poem should defeat the cruelty. . . ."

A corroboration of our interpretation, both of Providence and providential meaning to be stressed in the peculiar value of the verb, can be found in the *Monarchia* (II, ix, 19) when Dante states that the Roman "imperium" *contigit* only to the Roman people ("Sed hoc [imperium] nulli contigit nisi Romano populo").

For proof of Dante's *certezza* and to understand the full meaning not only of Dante's hope, but also of the providential necessity of the Holy Roman Empire, we turn to *Paradiso* XXVII, 61–66, in which St. Peter states:

> Ma l'alta provedenza che con Scipio
> difese a Roma la gloria del mondo,
> soccorrà tosto, sì com'io concipio.

St. Peter, being the foremost representative of faith, paves the way for a complete understanding of the second most important word, *fede*, at the beginning of Canto XXV. St. Peter's indispensable examination of Dante's faith was dramatically put into relief for the first time by Ugo Foscolo[25] but it was incorrectly interpreted as a justification of a heretical Dantesque conclusion. Although Foscolo's point of view is suggestive, based, as it appears to be, on the two figures of Gioachino da Fiore and Siger of Brabant, it is enough to subscribe to the implication of Etienne Gilson: "The general economy of the poem demands that charity should be added to faith, and be its consummation, just as faith is added to reason and enlightens it."[26] In other words, faith acquired through reason, which makes possible the attainment of supreme Christian perfection, is the only way to reach

---

[24]Sarolli, *loc. cit.*, 669–671.

[25]*La Divina Commedia di Dante Allighieri*, ed. U. Foscolo (London, 1842), I, "Introduzione," 82.

[26]E. Gilson, *Dante the Philosopher*, trans. D. Moore (London, 1948), 188.

union with God and the contemplation of God as stated by St. Paul: "videmus nunc per speculum et in aenigmate" and "tunc autem facie ad faciem." This is not only the conclusion of the *Divina Commedia* but also the explicit declaration of Beatrice in the central lines of Canto XXV, when she says of Dante:

> però li è conceduto che d'Egitto
> vegna in Ierusalemme, *per vedere*,
> anzi che'l militar li sia prescritto.

>   (55–57; my italics)

If we now consider the verbs *vedere* and *militare*, we cannot fail to recognize the allusive and direct relationship between the two. As I have pointed out elsewhere, considering Dante as the "scribe of God," I incline to the belief that *anzi che'l militar* does not mean "His soldiering on earth has yet to run,"[27] where soldiering endures for life, albeit "Christian life," *militia christiana*, but on the contrary means a positive task, a *militia litteraria*, with a causal relationship between *vedere* and *militar*; his Christian hope, arising from faith in God, was so strong in him that he was sure that he had been granted by grace alone the great vision and mission. With this in mind, we become fully aware of the meaning of the beginning of Canto XXV where, for the second time, Dante defines the *Divina Commedia* as a *poema* and adds *sacro* and "al quale ha posto mano e cielo e terra." We understand better also the very beginning of the poem when the verb *ritornare* appears at a most important moment, the moment when Dante has been stopped by the beasts and Virgil asks him: "Ma tu perché *ritorni* a tanta noia? (*Inf*. I, 76; my italics). This first anabasis to the *selva*, this renunciation of victory over the beasts even after the arrival of Virgil—not a saviour (although so invoked: *Miserere di me*, a direct translation of the beginning of Psalm 50, *Miserere mei*, the psalm of David's repentance) but a guide who will move the poet first away (*anabasis*) from God ("A te convien tenere altro viaggio" (*Inf*. I, 91; 112–144), and then toward (*katabasis*) Him—enables us to telescope the *Divina Commedia* also through the epic genre,[28] but in a kind of antitypical way. All the heroes of the chivalrous

[27]*The Comedy of Dante Alighieri, the Florentine*: III, *Paradise* ("Il Paradiso"), trans. Dorothy L. Sayers (Penguin Books), XXV, 58. Miss Sayers' translation can be considered as the last in the line of the traditional commentaries.

[28]Jessie L. Weston, *From Ritual to Romance* (New York, 1957).

tradition have beasts to defeat, are lost in a forest, and receive the advice of a hermit, those "Arturi regis ambages pulcerrime" so defined by Dante in his *De Vulgari Eloquentia* (I, x, 2).[29]

I shall not draw a direct parallel between the "epic landscapes," the *topos* studied by Curtius, in Dante and the romances of chivalry, for it would be only a superficial parallel. As a matter of fact, the hero of the chivalrous tradition proves himself in a task "pour briller devant sa dame" or "à la recherche de la vrai chevalerie," to quote Reto R. Bezzola.[30] But Dante does not willingly accept his task, does not defeat the beasts, and does not follow the invitation of Virgil, until Virgil has completely proved that Dante's journey has been decided by God as a providential mission. Still the chivalrous impact and vocabulary can easily be perceived, here and throughout the *Divina Commedia*, if we remember that Dante in the struggle between his will and his unwillingness labelled his task as an *impresa*:

> E qual è quei che disvuol ciò che volle
> e per novi pensier cangia proposta,
> sì che dal cominciar tutto si tolle,

> tal mi fec'io in quell'oscura costa,
> perché, pensando, consumai la'mpresa
> che fu nel cominciar cotanto tosta.   (*Inf.* II, 37–42)

There is also another aspect of the chivalrous tradition which can be taken into consideration, that of the quest for the Holy Grail[31] and the classical and mediaeval heritage of poetry related to Orpheus. The same twofold goal that appears in mediaeval Orphic lore,[32] the typological Orpheus/Christ : Euridice/Soul and the allegorical:

sì come quando dice Ovidio che Orfeo facea con la cetera mansuete le fiere, e li arbori e le pietre a se muovere; che vuol dire che lo savio uomo con lo strumento de la sua voce faria mansuescere e umiliare li crudeli cuori, e faria muovere a la sua volontade coloro che non hanno vita di scienza e d'arte (*Conv.* II, i, 3)

---

[29]On this point see the well-known article of P. Rajna in *Studi Danteschi*, I (1920), 31–42.

[30]Reto R. Bezzola, *Le sens de l'aventure et de l'amour: Chrétien de Troyes* (Paris, 1947), 158, 164.

[31]Frederick W. Locke, *The Quest for the Holy Grail* (Stanford, 1960).

[32]The mediaeval and Renaissance interpretation of the classical myth of Orpheus, expressed typologically in the equation Orpheus / Christ and morally in the identification of Eurydice with the human soul or reason is clearly and brilliantly epitomized by Wasserman in the article cited above.

is present also in Dante, although differentiated and enlarged. But while Orpheus will deal only with *descensus ad inferos*, Dante's journey will lead to his reunion with Beatrice (which is not the ultimate end) and to the accomplishment of what has been written in the *Vita Nuova* (XIX, 8–from the Canzone: "Donne ch'avete intelletto d'amore," 27–28) as an evident anticipation of the journey and of the *Divina Commedia*:

> (là'v'è alcun che perder lei s'attende,)
> e che dirà ne lo inferno: O mal nati,
> io vidi la speranza de'beati,

that is, Beatrice, on Earth already *speranza de'beati*.[33]

These brief references to the chivalrous and classical sources in the *Divina Commedia*, although the latter have been studied exhaustively by Renucci,[34] are introduced here, especially the former, as hypotheses for further future elaboration, and also, above all, because they are in a way related not only to the special journey of the poet but also to the particular and unique role of the poet, who is at the same time the protagonist and the author of the *Commedia*. The twofold identity of the poet, emphasized, with his usual insight, by Contini,[35] leads to a discussion of the double chronology of the journey and of an amendment of the punctuation marks advanced in the text.

I have the impression that Dante scholars, at least all those who accept Rodolico's explanation of the words *con altra voce* and *con altro vello*, have forgotten that the two chronologies can be correlated; in other words *altra voce* and *altro vello* cannot be references *sic et simpliciter* to the aging of the poet, as Rodolico very ingenuously claims:

nel primo dei tre versi distinguo il significato letterale dal figurato; intenderei letteralmente espressi gli effetti della sopravvenuta vecchiezza per l'affievolirsi della voce e l'incanutire dei capelli, immagine quest'ultima che in simile argomento ricorre nei versi dell'egloga dantesca in risposta a Giovanni del Virgilio; e nel significato figurato credo alluda al nuovo genere di poesia e alla nuova veste di poeta civile e religioso, non che

---

[33]This hypothesis was advanced by the poet G. Pascoli in his *Minerva Oscura, Prolegomeni: la costruzione morale del poema di Dante* (Livorno, 1898), 23.

[34]P. Renucci, *Dante disciple et juge du monde gréco-latin* (Paris, 1954).

[35]G. Contini, "Dante come personaggio-poeta della *Commedia*," in *Approdo*, IV (1958), pp. 19–46; also in *Libera Cattedra, Secoli vari ('300–'400–'500)* (Florence, 1958), 21–48.

alla nuova missione con cui sarebbe tornato in Firenze. La confusione dei due sensi, letterale e figurato, ha qui dato luogo ad un'arruffata matassa nei commentatori, dei quali vi risparmio le lunghe noiose e discordi opinioni.

Unfortunately, Rodolico, rather than disentangling the gnarled skein, has only succeeded in complicating it further. His was an error of perspective consisting in the failure to perceive that the *Eclogue* to G. del Virgilio has only an apparent bearing on the double chronology. This interpretation was accepted slavishly and indeed carried even further by Sapegno, who, in his edition of the *Divina Commedia*, commented:

... mutate dagli anni la voce e le chiome. Non occorre attribuire a voce e a vello un valore *meramente figurato*; come vogliono il Porena, il Torraca e il Grabher (e neppure, come pensano altri, alla voce sola); tutta la frase significherà: invecchiato ormai e canuto; e si capisce che il passar degli anni l'avrá maturato anche come poeta e come uomo, porgendo una materia di gran lunga piú vasta alla sua ispirazione e arricchendo il suo animo di saggezza e di prudenza.

However, when we read Porena's explanation,[36] Sapegno's statement does not appear to have added much to our understanding:

che altro vello abbia anche senso proprio e possa accennare anche al mutato colore dei capelli, non credo; che allora anche con altra voce dovrebbe avere un senso proprio, il che non è possibile: da trentasei a poco più di cinquant'anni un uomo non cambia voce!

It is my firm conviction, and fortunately not only mine, as will appear later on, that the literal interpretations of *voce* and *vello* presented thus far are by no means satisfactory. The claim made by Dante himself that his mission is that of a "scriba Dei" can throw some light on the metaphorical and allegorical meaning of the lines in question. The literal meaning of the verse, as it appears in Rodolico's gloss, cannot be justified by quoting Dante's *Eclogue* to G. del Virgilio, written in 1320 at the twilight of Dante's life, because it disrupts the correlation between the poet as author and as man; and secondly, it overlooks the possibility that the verse "nimico ai lupi che li danno guerra," inserted between the verse "del bello oville ov'io dormi'agnello" and "con altra voce omai, con altro vello," is ambivalent and less appropriate if related to the *agnello* than to the *new animal*, thus permitting

36*La Divina Commedia*, ed. M. Porena (Bologna, 1956), *Par.* XXV, *s.v.* "vello."

a change of the *terminus a quo* from 1300 to a more or less long time before, but in any case during *la prima etade*, as defined by the poet in *Convivio* (IV, iii, 126; xxiii, xxiv, 3 *passim*), when the literal *sensus* fits and paves the way to allegorical, according to the exegetical rule stated by Dante himself (both in *Conv.* II, i, 8, and in Can Grande's *Epistola* XII, 20). Nor can the other line, "sì che m'ha fatto per più anni macro," indicate only the duration of Dante's greatest poetic work. In fact we must not forget that the poet at the end of the *Vita Nuova* (XLII, 2) stated:

E di venire a ciò [that is, più degnamente trattare di lei—Beatrice] *io studio quanto posso, sì com'ella sae veracemente. Sì che, se piacere sarà di colui a cui tutte le cose vivono, che la mia vita duri per alquanti anni, io spero di dicer di lei quello che mai non fue detto d'alcuna.*

Thus we cannot eliminate the possibility that Dante, quoting those years, had had in mind the very years of preparation before the journey. In order to understand the full meaning of these words, we have only to agree with Charles S. Singleton on "the poetic ambiguity" implied in Dante's poetry, as the only rule left to Dante criticism, in order to capture the uni-plurality of the journey of the poet, which is at the same time our own journey taking place, "as to time, in a kind of ever present with every man as actor."[37] As we know, Singleton, basing his *lectura Dantis* on Biblical exegesis, points out the constant twofold aspect of Dante's poem, an aspect pointed out, although in a different way, by Auerbach[38] as well, and recently by Chydenius,[39] with the typical interpretation.[40] I shall go further, and by applying

[37]Charles S. Singleton, *Dante Studies I: Commedia, Elements of Structure*; II: *Journey to Beatrice* (Cambridge, Mass., 1953; 1958). From these two, already classic, studies, I have also borrowed the definition of Dante's poetry as "God's way of writing."

[38]From the first article, "Figura," in *Archivum Romanicum* XXII (1938), 436–489, to *Mimesis. Dargestellte Wirklichkeit in der abendländischen Literatur* (Bern, 1956); Erich Auerbach has based his interpretation of every mediaeval or Renaissance text on the alleged century-old typological interpretation. His theory can undoubtedly be considered, along with that of Singleton as the new highly fruitful way opened to Dante studies.

[39]J. Chydenius, *The Typological Problem in Dante: A Study in the History of Medieval Ideas* (Helsingfors, 1958).

[40]A recent, extremely important, *mise-à-point* of "The Problem of Literary Interpretation Reconsidered" in *Orbis Litterarum*, IV (1964), 66–76, by Helmut A. Hatzfeld, offers certainly a long-awaited basis and occasion for an international debate on Dante's *accessus*, in order to discuss deeply and freely the validity of past and present viewpoints.

one of the basic principles of Biblical exegesis, the *concordantia* and the "parallelism," consisting of the investigation of the constant reappearance in the Testaments of the same problematic passages hidden in one book but openly declared in another and designed to convey the analogical circularity of God's true message (*cf.* "Unde ea, quae in uno loco Scripturae traduntur sub metaphoris, in aliis locis expressius exponuntur," *Summa Theol.* I, 1, 9, ad 2), we can unfold the Dantesque "God's way of writing." Analogously, we can catch the monolithic polymorphy of the *Divina Commedia* by finding in the same canto, or elsewhere in the works of Dante, a recurrence of the same richly allusive value present in the two words *voce* and *vello*.

Voce appears several times in the *Divina Commedia* but it assumes a striking significance when it is related to Dante's journey and prophecy by Cacciaguida. To Dante's queries:

> Giù per lo mondo sanza fine amaro,
> e per lo monte del cui cacume
> li occhi de la mia donna mi levaro,
>
> e poscia per lo ciel di lume in lume,
> ho io appreso quel che s'io ridico,
> a molti fia sapor di forte agrume;
>
> e s'io al vero son timido amico,
> temo di perder viver tra coloro
> che questo tempo chiameranno antico.
>
> (*Par.* XVII, 112–120)

Cacciaguida replies:

> . . . Coscienza fusca
> o de la propria o de l'altrui vergogna
> pur sentirà la tua parola brusca.
>
> Ma nondimen, rimossa ogni menzogna,
> tutta tua vision fa manifesta;
> e lascia pur grattar dov'è la rogna.
>
> Che se la voce tua sarà molesta
> nel primo gusto, vital nutrimento
> lascerà poi, quando sarà digesta.
>
> Questo tuo grido farà come vento,
> che le più alte cime più percuote;
> e ciò non fa d'onor poco argomento.
>
> (*Par.* XVII, 124–135)

In this passage, *voce* is not only connected with *visione* but, as a result of the *repetitio*, it also becomes *grido*, thus implying the idea of strength and power which is so characteristic of the tradition of the prophets and particularly of Isaiah, "evangeli praenuntiator" as St. Thomas Aquinas described him.[41]

The passage of Isaiah 49 corroborates this view:

Super montem excelsum ascende tu qui evangelizas Sion: exalta in forti-tudine vocem tuam qui evangelizas Jerusalem: exalta, noli timere, dic civitatibus Judae: ecce Deus vester; ecce Dominus Deus in fortitudinem veniet, et brachium eius dominabitur; ecce merces eius cum eo.

By a close reading of the many glosses of the exegetical tradition and those collected by St. Thomas Aquinas, we can easily understand why this excerpt from Isaiah is so significant. St. Chrysostom (*Chrysos-tomus in Hom. sup. Matth.* [1, "non remote al principio"]) stated:

Quid enim his bonis nuntiatis fiat aequale Deus in terra, homo in coelo, amicitia Dei ad nostram facta naturam, prolixum solutum proelium, Diabolus confusus, mors soluta, Paradisus apertus. Et haec omnia super dignitatem nostram, et cum facilitate nobis data sunt; non quia laboravi-mus, sed quia dilecti sumus a Deo.

St. Augustine, moreover, in order to confirm the necessity of a scribe for God, said: "cur ipse Dominus nihil scripserit, ut aliis de ipso scribentibus, necesse sit credere. . . . Quicquid enim de suis factis et dictis nos legere voluit, hoc scribendum illis tamquam suis manibus imperavit."[42]

And, finally, the *Glossa Ordinaria*,[43] commenting on the sentence "exalta in fortitudine vocem tuam," reads "In quo etiam modum evangelicae doctrinae designat in exaltatione vocis, per quam doctrinae claritas datur." Obviously then, these passages of the Prophet Isaiah and of the exegetical tradition are intrinsic elements in the polyphonic richness of Dante's mind, and the whole range of associations with which this particular use of the word *voce* is pregnant can be ex-plained, as well as the real meaning of the second line of Canto XXV: "il poema sacro / a cui ha posto mano e cielo e terra." Among the Prophets, Isaiah is the one whose words have been very frequently

---

[41]See St. Thomas Aquinas, *Catena Aurea*, viz. *Expositio continua in Matth., Mc., Lc., Joa.*, ed. Fiaccadori (photostat., reprint by Musurgia; New York, 1949), I, xxxi.
[42]*Ibid.*, loc. cit. et *passim.*
[43]*Patrologia Latina* 113, col. 1291.

quoted by the exegetical tradition, and it is significant that his name appears in the same canto (91–93):

> Dice Isaia che ciascuna vestita
> nella sua terra fia di doppia vesta;
> e la sua terra è questa dolce vita.

Nor must we forget that Isaiah again is quoted in the *Epistola* VI (to the "scelestissimis Florentinis intrinsecis") when Henry VII is descibed as a *typus Christi*: ". . . ad ipsum, post Christum, digitum prophetiae propheta Isaias, quum, Spiritu Dei revelante, praedixit: 'Vere languores nostros ipse tulit, et dolores nostros ipse portavit' " (Isaiah 50:4), and also in other passages of other *Epistole*, along with other prophets. It is evident now that in Isaiah, the prophet of the salvation and liberation of Israel, and in the prophets in general and the prophetic context, must be found the answer to the obscure meaning of the other word *vello*, because the two appear interdependent. For the time being it is enough to quote, from Isaiah 61—the same chapter from which Dante has derived the three lines cited above—the following:

Spiritus Domini super me, eo quod unxerit Dominus me; ad annuntiandum mansuetis misit me, ut mederer contritis corde, et praedicarem captivis indulgentiam, et clausis apertionem; ut praedicarem . . . diem ultionis Deo nostro; ut consolarer omnes lugentes. . . .

And further on:

Gaudens gaudebo in Domino, et exultabit anima mea in Deo meo, quia induit me vestimentis salutis, et indumento justitiae circumdedit me.

And also, from Isaiah 50:3:

Dominus debit mihi linguam eruditam, ut sciam sustentare eum qui lapsus est, verbo.

Leaving aside all the details of the glosses of the Biblical tradition, and those collected by Thomas Aquinas, let us summarize by saying that on this particular point the *Angelicus Doctor* pointed out the perfection of Holy Scriptures and that Jerome emphasized the soteriological implication by glossing: "Dicit enim se a Domino accepisse sermonem, quomodo lapsum errantemque populum sustentet, et revocit ad salutem"; a gloss which indeed seems not too far from the many commands by Beatrice and St. Peter to Dante to repeat again and again the words he has been told or he has heard, and we can say the same about the admonition of Cacciaguida. If all these references can relate the word *voce* to the prophecy, let us determine if in the same exegetical tradition there is an analogical reference to the word *vello*.

Vello, as we know, is a word very seldom used by Dante, in the *Divina Commedia* only three times (*Inf.* XXXIV, 74; *Par.* VI, 108; *Par.* XXV, 7), and only once in the *Eclogues* (*Eclog.* II, 1) and that in relation to the Argonauts. In all these cases the meaning of the word cannot be an equivalent of "hair" and it is important to underline this point. This can be proved even in the Lucifer description (*Inf.* XXXIV, 74) where the word *vello* is repeated twice, immediately before the other word *pelo* (utilized by the poet elsewhere to mean hair —*Par.* IX, 99: ". . . infin che si convenne al pelo") showing openly a clear-cut difference between the two expressions, and implying that Lucifer has not only three faces but also three fleeces. The passage certainly deserves further consideration. But the best example is the last one, that of the *Eclogue* (II, 1: "Velleribus Colchis praepe detectus Eous") because here the poet, by synecdoche, used *vellus* for the animal, as in the Jason episode, "li Colchi del monton privati fene," in the *Divina Commedia* (*Inf.* XVIII, 87) he used the name of the ram (*monton*) where we were expecting to find the term "Golden Fleece," well known not only through Ovid in the *Metamorphoses* (VII, 1–158) and Virgil's brief statement (*Eclog.* IV, 31), but also through contamination with the Biblical *vellus Gedeonis* (Judges 6:37).

We know that the Christian exegetical tradition worked out the Biblical episode, beginning with Jerome (*Ad Paulinum*),[44] who stated:

Postquam siccato vellere universus orbis coelesti rore perfuses est, et multi de Oriente et Occidente venientes recubuerunt in sinu Abrahae, dessit esse notus tantum in Judaea Deus et in Israel magnum nomen ejus, sed in omnem terram exivit sonus apostolorum, et in fines orbis terrae verba eorum.

Augustine (*De Unitate Ecclesiae* V)[45] first underlined the allegorical viewpoint, and Ambrose (*De Viduis*)[46] initiated the typological approach with the equation Vellus/Virgin Mary which was later

44*Ibid.* 28, col. 175.   45*Ibid.* 43, col. 391.   46*Ibid.* 16, col. 233.

emphasized, as the end of a long succession of Fathers and Doctors of the Church, by St. Bernard in his *Sermones* (*In Nativ. Mariae*: "Intuere, o homo, consilium Dei, agnosce consilium sapientiae, consilium pietatis. Coelesti rore aream rigaturus, totum vellus prius infudit; redempturus humanum genus, pretium universum contulit in Mariam").[47]

This exegetical tradition was considered from a different angle by St. Thomas Aquinas and was questioned in his *Summa Theol.* (II, II, *Quaest*. XCVII, art. 2, *ad* 3), that is, whether Gideon did or did not sin when he asked for a second *signum* from God (". . . et nonnulli alii censent Gedeonem peccasse infidelitate, vel mortali, vel saltem veniali, eo quod dubitarit de promissis Dei, ac ab eo ex debilitate fidei novum signum petierit"). Although we are not concerned with the question, it is important to underline the fact that as late as Nicholas of Lyre, the Franciscan Biblical commentator of the beginning of the fourteenth century, we find Gideon absolved of the sin, and the *signum* itself considered, following the previous commentators, a *signum victoriae*.

But it is especially in the *Aurora*, the *Biblia versificata*, the most popular verse Bible or verse commentary on the Bible in the Middle Ages (late twelfth-century) of Peter Riga, that there is a unified résumé of the whole Biblical and exegetical tradition, "for in many respects it is similar to the prose commentaries from which much of its material was extracted, condensed, or paraphrased":[48]

(*Liber Iudicum, De Gedeone*)
> Exorat fieri Gedeon in uellere signum
> Ut di deuincat hostica bella sciat.
> Vellus compluitur, rorem sitit area: uellus
> Iudeam, gentes arida signat humus;
> Legis nube Deus prius irrorauit Hebreos,
> Sed fuit a tanto gens aliena bono.
> Signum mutatur: fusum bibit area rorem,
> Lana sitim patitur que fuit uda prius:
> Sic sua dona Deus in nos conuertit, Hebreos
> Ieiunos patiens muneris esse sui.

---

[47]*Ibid*. 183, col. 840.
[48]*Aurora, Petri Rigae Biblia Versificata* ed. Paul E. Beichner, C.S.C. (Notre Dame, Ind., 1965), I, xi.

Concha repletur aquis expresso uellere: concham
Virginis implesti munere, Christe, tuo.
His Gedeon signis certus de laude triumphi
Innumero cinctus milite flumen adit. . . .   (105–118)

Finally, it must not be forgotten that from Eusebius (*Chronic.*) to
Peter Comestor there is the idea that the episode of Gideon was
considered the source of the Argonauts' legend: "Denique ex hox
Gedeonis vellere orta est historia vel fabula Argonautarum, qui
sexaginta annis post Gedeonem sub Abesan Judice floruisse . . .
Hi [the Argonauts] enim fuere LIV heroes, qui in navi dicta Argo
navigarunt in Colchum, ut vellus aureum auferrent. . . ."[49]

Such a widely diffused and well-known tradition linked to the
Gideon episode was later accepted and hallowed in the liturgy,
particularly in the coronation ceremony, when in one of the Bishop's
prayers we read: "Visita eum sicut Moysen in rubo, Iesum Nave
in praelio, *Gedeon in agro*, Samuelum in templo et illa eum benedic-
tione syderae ac sapientiae tuae rore perfunde, quam beatus David
in psalterio, Salomon filius ejus te renumerante percepit e coelo. . . ."
(my italics)[50]

Thus it should no longer be surprising not to find the synecdochal
"Golden Fleece" in the Jason episode in the *Divina Commedia*, but
the name of the animal, the ram, the animal which appears in
Landino's allegorical *Comment* on the *Divina Commedia* as an
explanation of the word *vello*: ". . . con altro vello, stette nella
traslatione, quasi dica, non con vello d'agnello, ma di robusto mon-
tone."[51]

[49]To be considered, along with its *Interpretatio* (*Patrologia Latina* 27, col. 34 ff.)
by St. Jerome, a kind of common basis for the other historical synopses and elaboration up to the *Speculum Regum* by Godfrey of Viterbo and Peter Comestor's
Historia Scolastica ("Argonotarum historia facta est Orphaeus clarus habitus est,"
P.L. 198, col. 1281).

[50]M. Andrieu, *Le pontifical romain au moyen âge*: I, *Le pontifical romain au
XIIe siècle*, 251, 253 ("Ordo ad benedicendum imperatorem," and "ad suscipiendam
coronam imperii"); II, *Le pontifical de la curie romaine au XIIIe siècle*, pp. 382,
388; III, *Le pontifical de Guillaume Durand*, p. 429 ("Ordo romanus ad benedicendum regem vel reginam, imperatorem vel imperatricem"); in *Studi e testi*, vols. 86,
87, 88 (Rome, 1938–1940).

[51]*Dante*, con l'espositioni di Christoforo Landino et d'Alessandro Vellutello, *Sopra
la sua Comedia dell'Inferno, del Purgatorio, et del Paradiso*, con tavole . . . . et
ridotto alla sua vera lezione per Francesco Sansovino Fiorentino (Venice, 1578),
fol. 364r.

The equation, Vellus Gedeonis/Virgin Mary appears in the
Laborintus, the didactic poem on rhetoric, of Eberhard the German:[52]

> Nomina nominibus se concubina maritant.
> Ad Christi matrem sic modulare piam:
> *Aaron virga, rubus Moysi, lampas paradisi,*
>   *Caeli porta, decus virginitatis, ave!*
> *Funda David, radix Jesse, vellus Gedeonis,*
>   *Pacifici solium, foederis archa, vale!*   (735–740)

If my interpretation of *vello* and its metaphorical implications, or
merely its meaning as a *signum victoriae,* are correct, any further
inference can only be that *vello* as a synecdoche for ram is not quite
acceptable, even though it is a synecdoche. It is necessary to find out
what animal is rhetorically expressed through the word *vello.*

Of course our inference is based upon the fact that the poet knew
the two episodes, that of Gideon:

> e delli Ebrei ch'al ber si mostrar molli,
>   per che no i volle Gedeon compagni,
>   quando ver Madian discese i colli
> (Purg. XXIV, 124–126),

and that of Jason:

> Quelli è Iason, che per cuore e per senno
> li Colchi del monton privati fene.
>
> Ello passò per l'isola di Lenno,
>   poi che l'ardite femmine spietate
>   tutti li maschi loro a morte dienno . . .
>
> Ivi con segni e con parole ornate
>   Isifile ingannò, la giovinetta
>   che prima avea tutte l'altre ingannate.
>
> Lasciolla quivi, gravida, soletta;
>   tal colpa a tal martiro lui condanna;
>   e anche di Medea si fa vendetta.   (*Inf.* XVIII, 86–96).

There is another example in *Paradiso* II, 16–18:

> Que' gloriosi che passaro al Colco
>   non s'ammiraron come voi farete,
>   quando Iason vider fatto bifolco[53]

---

[52]Faral (*supra* note 13), 363.
[53]To these verses, object of a highly *vexata quaestio,* I will return in another article.

where the verb *ammirare* appears contrapuntally crossbred, from Ovid's *Metamorphoses* VII, 118–121:

> Suppositosque jugo pondus grave cogit aratri
> Ducere, et insuetum ferro proscindere campum.
> *Mirantur* Colchi; *Miniae* clamoribus implent,
> Adjiciuntque animos. . . . (my italics)

Dante's bestiary, the animal world in the *Divina Commedia*, represented by ninety-three specimens (the total number is one hundred and eleven but I am not including the very interesting variations of a single specimen used in its diminutive or augmentative or mixed form), offers a wide selection of sources, from the classical and mythical heritage to Christian allegorization, and to common knowledge, all characterized by the names of animals, expressed either by Latinisms or by Romance forms, Italian or French; it also demonstrates a very important peculiarity, namely that all the animals carrying an allegorical or metaphorical meaning are used more than once (with the exception of the very christological ones). It is an old rhetorical device but nevertheless in the *Divina Commedia*, which is at once "logical and imaginative" and "an extraordinary fusion of rhetoric and poetic,"[54] the poet operates in his unique way. The best example perhaps is the very subtle distinction between *pecore* and *agni* as it appears in *Paradiso* (IX, 127–132):

> La tua città, che di colui è pianta
>   che pria volse le spalle al suo fattore
>   e di cui è la'nvidia tanto pianta,
>
> produce e spande il maladetto fiore
>   c'ha disviate le *pecore* e li *agni*,
>   però che fatto ha lupo del pastore. (my italics)

This distinction, overlooked by the most recent commentators, interpreted by the ancient ones metaphorically as "ogni condizione di persone" (Vellutello), "i grandi e i piccini" (Landino), is indeed very significant if we follow the steps of our poet not only in the *Divina Commedia* but also in the other works: in *Convivio* (I, i, 7: "Oh beati quelli pochi che seggiono a quella mensa dove lo pane de

---

[54]Charles S. Baldwin, *Medieval Rhetoric and Poetic (to 1400)* (Gloucester, Mass., 1959), 277.

li angeli si manuca! e miseri quelli che con le pecore hanno comune cibo!"; and also I, xi, 9–10; II, vii, 4–5: ". . . e non dico pur de le minori bestie, ma di quelle che hanno *apparenza umana* e *spirito di pecora*"); in *Monarchia* (III, xv, 3–4: "Forma autem Ecclesie nihil aliud est quam vita Christi, tam in dictis quam in factis comprehensa: vita enim ipsius ydea fuit et exemplar militantis Ecclesie, presertim *pastorum maxime summi,* cuius est *pascere agnos et oves*") where he expresses, in almost the same words, the idea of the passage from the *Paradiso*; in *Epistola* V, 87: ("universis et singulis Ytalie. . . .": "Parcite, parcite iam ex nunc, o carissimi, qui mecum iniuriam passi estis, ut *Hectoreus pastor* vos *oves* de *ovili suo* cognoscat. . . .") where once more Henry VII is declared to be the *typus-Christi,* according to the formula of political theology, elsewhere widely discussed; in *Epistola* VII, 10 ("Sanctissimo gloriosissimo atque felicissimo triumphatori. . . .": "Tunc exultavit in te spiritus meus, cum tacitus dixi mecum: 'Ecce agnus Dei, ecce qui tollit peccata mundi' "; 18: "Iohannes namque, regius primogenitus tuus et rex . . . in Turnos ubique sicut *leo* deseviet et in Latinos velut *agnus* mitescet"); and in *Epistola* XI, 9 ("Cardinalibus ytalicis. . . .": "Quippe de *ovibus* pascue Iesu Christi minima una sum; quippe nulla pastorali auctoritate abutens, quoniam divitie mecum non sunt"). In these works, then, *pecora,* the "vulgar" form, always implies a lower degree; it is pejorative, while *agni* has the same meaning either in "vulgar" or in "Latin" and implies a higher degree of evaluation; consequently I conclude that *pecora* stands for *ovis, in malo* as opposed to *agnello, in bono* (a distinction that goes back to St. Isidore, *Etym.* XII, i, 6).

Perhaps it is now possible to draw a preliminary conclusion to clarify, to a certain extent, the position of the word *vello.* When Dante calls himself *agnello,* which stands for *ovis,* he implies clearly enough that he is the follower of both Christ ("de ovibus pascue Iesu Christi minima una sum") and the Emperor—*typus-Christi*—("ut Hectoreus pastor vos oves de ovili suo cognoscat") because *agno* is used in the *Divina Commedia* to refer to higher ranks exclusively, as in *Paradiso* X, 94: "Io fui degli *agni* della santa greggia," where the speaker is St. Thomas Aquinas, and in *Epistola* VII, 18: "Iohannes namque, regius primogenitus tuus et rex . . . in Latinos velut *agnus* mitescet," where he is referring to John of Bohemia.

Thus, since *vello* means "fleece" and not "hair," when Dante writes "con altro vello" he must imply a "fleece" different from that of an *agnello*. It must be one that, by analogy, carries an allegorical meaning related to the prophecy, as a counter-part of the *altra voce*. Now the only animal which fulfills our requirement, according to the *Bestiaries* and the *Distinctiones dictionum theologicalium* of Alan of Lille,[55] is the *caprea* (goat).

In fact, under the item *caprea* we read that Christ is "capreae similatur secundum divinitatem" because of the goat's property of secreting a humour which, according to medical treatises, removes film from the eyes and thus improves the eyesight. Alan of Lille, moreover, compares the prophets to the "capreae propter profeticam revelationem, quia sicut caprea subtilem habet visum, ita profeta in praevidendis futuris subtilem habet intellectum." This, of course, is mere external evidence which to be valid must be supported by internal evidence.

In the whole *Divina Commedia* Dante compares himself directly with one animal only, to be precise, with a *capra*, and in a very commonplace way, that is, before a sleep, but a sleep—to quote Dante— "che sovente,/anzi che'l fatto sia, sa le novelle" (*Purg.* XXVII, 92–93), in other words, a prophetic dream:[56]

> Quali si stanno ruminando manse
> le capre, state rapide e proterve
> sovra le cime avante che sien pranse,
>
> tacite all'ombra, mentre ch'l sol ferve,
> guardate dal pastor, che'n su la verga
> poggiato s'è e lor poggiato serve;
>
> e quale il mandrian che fori alberga,
> lungo il peculio suo queto pernotta,
> guardando perché fiera non lo sperga;

[55]*Patrologia Latina* 210, col. 685.

[56]Nor should we overlook St. Isidore's statement on the *capra* (*Etym.* I, xl: "Ad naturam rerum fabulas fingunt . . . ut illa triformis bestia; (Lucret. 5, 903) 'Prima leo, postrema draco, media ipsa chimaera'; id est caprea, aetate hominum per eam volentes distinguere; quarum ferox et horreus prima adolescentia, ut leo; *dimidium vitae tempus lucidissimum, ut caprea, eo quod acutissime videat*; tunc fit senectus casibus inflexis, draco.") in which we can identify the original source of the long tradition which culminated not only in Alan of Lille, but also in the glossarial lore divided in two parts, *in bono* and *in malo*. Only the second one has been taken into account by George Ferguson's *Signs and Symbols in Christian Art* (New York, n.d.), 6. The second possible suggestion in St. Isidore's statement, that is, the relationship *caprea/aetas hominum* (*dimidium vitae*), although suggestive if compared with the *mezzo del cammino* of Dante-mankind-life, seems less probable.

tali eravam noi tutti e tre allotta,
io come capra, ed ei come pastori,
fasciati quinci e quindi d'alta grotta.
                            (*Purg.* XXVII, 76–87; my italics)[57]

This beautiful pastoral metaphor gives the key to understanding
the wide range of implications that the word *vello* holds, and at the
same time strengthens the relationship between Dante and Alan of
Lille, whose works, and particularly the *Anticlaudianus, sive de officio
viri boni et perfecti*, have recently been included in the list of Dante's
sources.[58]

There is, in fact, a close relationship between the creation of the
perfect man by nature in the *Anticlaudianus* and Dante's own journey
toward perfection and the unique synthesis in his own person of all the
vices and virtues of mankind, implying the purification of mankind
with his own purification. Kantorowicz asserts that one of the important principles of political theology is "the problem of collective
guilt," often interpreted as a secular parallel of Original Sin with
which the totality of mankind, *universitas*, was charged as an indivi-
sible whole, a kind of unit which does not distinguish parts.

This statement is confirmed, although in different terms, by St.
Thomas Aquinas:

respondeo: Et ideo alia via procedendum est, dicendo quod omnes homines
qui nascuntur ex Adam, possunt considerari ut unus homo, in quantum
conveniunt in natura quam a primo parente accipiunt secundum quod in
civilibus omnes homines qui sunt unius communitatis, reputantur quasi
unum corpus, et tota communitas quasi unus homo. (*Summa theol.* I, ii,
q. 81, a. 1)

Without entering more deeply into this particular problem, which,
of course, can be referred diachronically to every century of the
Christian era and to the many varied ideas about man's renovation,
reformation, and regeneration, it is enough to underline the two

[57]It is evident that the broad allusion to the *agno* in the long simile of *Par.* IV,
1–12 can be referred to the poet only indirectly, and more directly to the poet as a
libero uomo, and in general to the *liberi uomini*, without the direct relevant relation
"Io come *capra*," which must be related clearly to the previously mentioned "Io
fui degli *agni*" (*Par.* X, 94) standing for St. Thomas Aquinas. The same, as above,
mutatis mutandis, for the "falcone" of *Purg.* XIX, 64.

[58]See the effective and suggestive article of Edward C. Witke, "The River of
Light in the *Anticlaudianus* and the *Divina Commedia*," in *Classical Review* XI
(1959), 144–156.

very basic points on which all Christian writers agreed. Here again let us quote Kantorowicz:

On the one hand it was the goal of every Christian, and of Christianity at large, to recover the original image of man such as it had been before the fall—created to the likeness of God a little lower than the angels. On the other hand, every believer was potentially elected, owing to the incarnation of the son of God, to participate in the divine nature of Christ and thereby to re-establish in himself also the original integrity of human nature, that is, the verisimilitude with God which had been bestowed upon the first man on the day of his making. In other words, the image of the paradisian Adam was merged in that of Christ, the new Adam; and the original God-likeness of Adam in paradise was, by the support of divine grace, recovered through Christ.[59]

Briefly, now, we can review the use Dante made of this particular tradition. St. Augustine, for one, considered regenerated man superior to Adam even as he was before the Fall.[60] Dante, on the contrary, in his re-humanizing of the idea of a recovery of Adam's original nature used a conception of the human which was different from the Christian tradition. He seems to believe in a concept of perfection in both a terrestrial and a celestrial Paradise, secularizing the Adam-theology and building up a doctrine of human regeneration valid both in Heaven and on earth through the world monarchy. In other words, he unifies the heavenly city, the Augustinian City of God, with the earthly city, rebuilding typologically the heavenly Trinity, God the father, Christ the son, and the Holy Spirit, in a terrestrial Trinity represented by the *Vicarii Dei*, the *typus-Christi*, and *Spiritui Sancti*, that is, the Pope, the Emperor, and the prophet-counsellor.[61]

I have already illustrated this idea in "Dante 'scriba Dei'" but I shall focus my attention once again on the unique manner adopted by Dante in considering all humanity, through the Orosian doctrine of Providence, as participating and descending in human nature from

[59]Kantorowicz, *The King's Two Bodies*, 476–478.

[60]See St. Augustine's conception of the reformation of man in the image of God, in *Augustinus magister* (Communications of the Congrès international augustinien, Paris, Sept., 1954).

[61]This trichotomy is, *mutatis mutandis*, the same as Gilson's (*op. cit.*, 188 ff.), and we owe it to his highly stimulating discussion of *Monarchia* III, 12. Against the trichotomy of Gilson, Kantorowicz (*op. cit.*, 461, n. 31) has opposed a dichotomy. Without denying validity to the counter-hypothesis, I still agree with Gilson, because from the *Monarchia* to the *Divina Commedia*, a Trinitarianism, in theological-political terms, is certainly not out of the question. But to this I will return later on.

Adam in a new sacral quality extended to the Greeks and Romans. With the Romans in fact, the prefiguration of Christ as the new Adam was achieved with Aeneas and Virgil, both standing for the Roman Empire and the *Pax Augusti* proclaimed in the very days of the Saviour's birth which was accompanied by the "Pax in coelis et in terris," sung by the angels.

This is the ground, the golden section, of the *Divina Commedia*; this is the unifying principle of heaven and earth, constantly present in the poem; here lies the explanation through which the line in our canto, "a cui ha posto mano e cielo e terra," finds its unequivocal explanation.

But once again, let us follow the anabasis-katabasis of Dante (to be referred to the traditional and well-known Pythagorean letter Y)[62] from and to God through the three canticles in order to understand better the nature of *libertà* which the poet "va cercando," as Virgil says to Cato at the gate of Purgatory, and in order to elucidate the final quandary of Canto XXV, that is, the word *cappello*, whose meaning is rendered uncertain by the presence of the reference to the font.

Hell and Purgatory, in the *Divina Commedia*, have the obvious function of demonstrating how Dante—man in general or all of mankind personified by the poet—was led by philosophy and secular wisdom from a sinful state back to the "natura sincera e buona" of the first man before the Fall (*Par.* VII, 35 ff.). To be sure, only the Church was competent to prepare man for his future spiritual immortality, since, as a remedy for the first transgression and the ensuing loss of corporeal immortality, the Church administered the sacrament of spiritual rebirth, baptism.

With this in mind, we can perhaps better understand why Dante in his katabasis "to earth" speaks of the "fonte del mio battesmo," where he will take "il cappello." This word *cappello* has been recently

---

[62]"Y litteram Pythagoras Samius ad exemplum vitae humanae primus formavit; cuius virgula subterior primam aetatem significat, incertam quippe et quae adhuc nec vitiis nec virtutibus dedit. Bivium autem, quod superest, ab adolescentia incipit: cuius dextra pars ardua est, sed ad beatam vitam tendens: sinistra facilior, sed ad labem interitumque deducens. De qua sic Persius ait (3, 56): 'Et tibi qua Samios deduxit littera ramos, / surgentum dextro mostravit limite callem" (Isidore, *Etym.* I, iii, 7). Isidore's statement was repeated again and again, became traditional, and was constantly quoted by the commentators of Virgil, especially Servius (*Ad Aen.* VI, 136) and Bernard Silvestris (*Super sex libros Eneidos Vergilii*, ed. G. Riedel), 12. On the problem left/right way in the *Divina Commedia*, it is imperative to consult the articles of John Freccero, especially "Infernal Inversion and Christian Conversion (*Inferno* XXXIV)" in *Italica*, XLII (1965), 35–41.

at the centre of an interesting polemic between Rossi and Padoan,[63] but its conclusion still does not satisfy us completely, because neither the theological *birretta* nor, literally speaking, the poetic *corona d'alloro* seems to fit properly in Dante's passage, complicated as it appears by the very problematic presence of the font. The four terms—*altra voce, altro vello, poeta, cappello*—if considered interrelated, appear linked together in a double duality, but not as hendiadys as we have already seen for the first two: *voce* and *vello*. For this reason, *cappello* as poetic "crown" will weaken the poetic image, and at the same time will make more evident and even emphasize Dante's own unilateral decision to take "the poetic crown with his hands." Once again we must turn to Dante's works to discover the special meaning he intends for these words.

Cappello is used only four times in the *Divina Commedia*: once metaphorically, in *Inferno* XXXII, 126: "sì che l'un capo a l'altro era cappello," and the other three literally, all in the *Paradiso*; (XIX, 34) "Quasi falcone ch'esce del cappello," (XXI, 125) "quando fui chiesto e tratto a quel cappello," and in the passage considered here. The second example from the *Paradiso* occurs in the episode of St. Peter Damian, and there *cappello* stands for a Cardinal's hat, a political-theological use, although at first glance it may appear a blasphemy, denying the well-established principle of Dante's orthodoxy.

But before entering into details, I shall quote the poet, and especially his *Epistle to the Cardinals*, described by Passerin d'Entrèves as the greatest of his *Epistole*. If we read the letter carefully we discover the extreme resourcefulness of the poet in using theological terminology, when he claims, with St. Paul, to be "de ovibus pascue Iesu Christi minima una. . . ." and, again with St. Paul (Cor. 15:10), St. John (8:58) and God himself (Exodus 3:14) "[Gratia Dei] sum id quod sum," and the Uzzah episode (II Samuel 6:6–7), where the prohibition against a layman intervening *in sacris* is stated in no uncertain terms—and we must not forget that the same episode is used as an example in *Purgatorio* X, 55–57:

> Era intagliato lì nel marmo stesso
> lo carro e i buoi, traendo l'arca santa,
> per che si teme officio non commesso.

---

[63]See A. Rossi, "Dante, Boccaccio e la laurea poetica," in *Paragone*, CL (1962), 3–41, and the review article by G. Padoan in *Studi sul Boccaccio*, I, ed. V. Branca (Florence, 1963), 517–540.

In equally certain terms Dante differentiates between himself and the Biblical figure by stating: "Nec Oze presumptio quam obiectandam quis crederet, quasi temere prorumpentem me sui tabe reatus; quia *ille ad arcam, ego ad boves calcitrantes* et, per abvia distrahentes attendo," (my italics) and concluding, fully aware of God's Providence: "Ille [God] ad arcam [the Church] proficiat qui salutiferos oculos ad naviculam fluctuantem aperuit." (*Ep.* XI, 9–12) No better evidence can be offered of the lack of heresy in Dante; indeed this is the best proof of the quasi-soteriological essence of his mission, especially if we consider the other episode where again the font appears in a disguised but distinguishable way:

> Non mi parean men ampi nè maggiori
>   che que' che son nel mio bel San Giovanni,
>   fatti per luogo de' battezzatori;
>
> l'un de li quali, ancor non molt'anni,
>   rupp'io per un che dentro v'annegava:
>   e questo sia suggel ch'ogn'uomo sganni.
>
> (Inf. XIX, 16–21)

To this particular point, repeatedly discussed by the commentators,[64] I will specifically return in another work, but, for the time being, I shall repeat the statement of Gilson: "The text of the *Divine Comedy* much rather suggests the idea that Dante is a moralist and reformer who arms himself with all the theses required for his work of reform and by his moral philosophy."[65] Indeed, this helps us to understand clearly why the poet considered it necessary and indispensable to insert the examination on Hope in Canto XXV, immediately after the examination on Faith and to underline it so strikingly through Beatrice's words and the Beatific Chorus, singing all around him the beautiful Psalm IX (11: "Sperent in te"), which is the very Psalm of the Victory.[66]

[64]But certainly nothing new and no clarification is added by a very recent article of Mark Musa on this difficult verse ("E questo sia suggel ch'ogn'uomo sganni" *Inf.* XIX, 21) in *Italica*, XLI (1964), 134–137, in which one of the central and most vexing problems of the *Divina Commedia* is superficially examined and considered solved. For the time being, the reader should consult David Knowles' article "A Characteristic of the Mental Climate of the Fourteenth Century," in *Mélanges* . . . *Gilson* (Toronto–Paris, 1959), 315–325, even though it bears on the subject only indirectly.

[65]Gilson, *Dante the Philosopher*, 276.

[66]For the entire tradition see Hugh of St. Cher, *Opera Omnia: In Psalmos*, IV (Lyons, 1645), f. 57r.

The presence of David's Psalm, along with the Prophet of the salvation of Israel, mentioned here for the first and only time, is certainly not accidental. It is enough to say that the political and theological implication is almost evident if we only consider that David and Solomon, particularly the latter, are the perfect kings. Typologically, they have been referred to as *figurae Christi* and consequently *figurae* of the Holy Roman Emperors. Let us remember, moreover, that Dante, as we have already demonstrated elsewhere, referred to Henry VII as a new David and Caesar and to his son, John of Bohemia, as a future second Solomon and Augustus, as well as to himself as a new Nathan, the prophet and scribe of David and Solomon, but also *tunc* and *sub specie aeternitatis*.

Now I shall consider the word *battesmo* and the twofold use the poet has made of the sacrament. In the *Purgatorio*, Virgil, answering the question of Sordello of Goito concerning the place where the Latin poet dwells, replies:

> Quivi [Limbo] sto io coi pargoli innocenti
> dai denti morsi della morte avante
> che fosser dall'umana colpa esenti;
>
> quivi sto io con quei che le tre sante
> virtù non si vestiro, e sanza vizio
> conobber l'altre e seguir tutte quante. (*Purg.* VII, 31–36)

This can be interpreted as: "I dwell both with those who have not been baptized [by the Church] and with those who 'did not put on' the three theological virtues"; again the sacrament, but in an *ab aeterno* way, the only one which will permit the salvation of Ripheus the Trojan, in *Paradiso* XX, 127:

> Quelle tre donne li fur per battesmo
> che tu vedesti da la destra rota,
> dinanzi al battezzar più d'un millesmo.

This is justified, in the following lines, as Predestination:

> O predestinazion, quanto remota
> è la radice tua da quelli aspetti
> che la prima cagion non veggion tota!

Only the Church can administer the first sacrament, that of Baptism, but, according to the mediaeval dualistic principle, there is a para-sacrament which is administered by the Empire. This sacrament can be considered an antitype which is somehow pre-existent to the historical sacrament administered by the Church. The identity of this para-sacramen can be discovered through a close study of Dante's text.

In the *Purgatorio*, when Dante was at the gate of Purgatory (IX, 19 ff.), he dreamed that Jupiter's eagle snatched him like another Ganymede up to the fiery sphere of heaven where both the eagle and the poet seemed to go up in flames: "a dream," says Kantorowicz[67] "of purification through the imperial (that is, moral-philosophic) power which here is compared also with the customary meaning of the eagle as a symbol of baptismal regeneration."

The golden eagles will reappear again, almost immediately, and in connection with the Empire, in the following canto (X, 73 ff.) in the famous episode of the carved relief of the Emperor Trajan, at which point appear two words indispensable for our inquiry: "justice and piety," which are the same words that the *M*, which is metamorphosed into an Eagle, will pronounce in *Paradiso* (XIX, 13 ff.): "per esser *giusto* e *pio*."[68] Here the Eagle is again related to Jupiter.

Justice, then, is that para-sacrament administered by the Empire, a justice, of course, which adhered to the principles of political theology so deeply and penetratingly discussed by Kantorowicz. This is not the place for a detailed analysis of these principles; it is enough to quote, in order to prove the point, the prologue of the *Quaestiones de iuris subtilitatibus* of Placentinus, where the author:

erected a literary monument of the goddesses of Law when describing, solemnly and in glowing colors, the beauty and majesty of the *Templum Justitiae*, which he pretended to have discovered, by chance, in a pleasant grove on the top of a hill. In that imaginary shrine he saw Reason, Justice, and Equity dwelling together with the six civic virtues—a "celestial banquet," so it seemed to him, rather than anything on earth. . . . Within the Shrine some space was reserved for the inaccessible Holy of Holies, the *adytum*, which was separated by a wall of glass on which, with golden letters, the full texts of Justinian's law books were inscribed. It was only through that glass wall that the spectator viewed the deities "as in a mirror." Inside the *adytum*, "a not too modest number of honorable men,"

---

[67]*The King's Two Bodies*, 487–488; see also Ferguson, *Signs and Symbols in Christian Art*, 5.

[68]Sarolli, "*Ingigliarsi all'emme* (*Par.* XVIII, 113): archetipo di poliunivoca concordanza," in *Atti del Congresso internazionale di Studi Danteschi*, II (Florence, 1965), 183–198.

apparently *the Clergy of Justice*, was in attendance at the glass wall, ever ready to revise the texts of the golden lettering whenever a passage appeared disarrayed to the examining eyes of law-weighing Equity. Outside the *adytum*, finally, a venerable teacher of Law discussed with his auditors difficult legal problems, and it was the discussion between this interpreter of the Law and his audience which the author of the *Quaestiones* pretended to reproduce in his learned tractate. (Kantorowicz, p. 109)

This representation of Justice and of the Temple, stimulated by Justinian's letter to Tribonian and also borrowed from Aulus Gellius' *Attic Nights*, who had reproduced from "Stoic sources a similar literary portrait of Iustitia, 'an awe-inspiring virgin with penetrating eyes and with some venerable grief in her dignity,' and attended by the perfect judge whom Gellius called *Iustitiae antistes*, 'the priest of Justice'," was repeated over and over again along with the sentence "Prius fuit Iustitia quam ius," which appears in all the glossators and will lead to the great prologue of the *Liber augustalis* of Frederick II. But in connection with the visionary Temple of Justice of Placentinus, attention has also been called to a miniature of an earlier date showing the emperor as mediator in legal matters.

The miniature is found in the magnificent Gospel book which Emperor Henry II, in 1022 or 1023, donated to the Abbey of Montecasino. The folio preceding the Fourth Gospel, where a representation of St. John would be expected, shows instead a full-page image of the emperor . . . enthroned in full regalia. In the upper corners we recognize *Iustitia* and *Pietas*; to the right and left, placed in smaller circles, are *Sapientia* and *Prudentia*, attendants and throne companions of kingship since earliest times. In the corners below the ruler are *Lex* and *Ius*, the symbols of Positive Law. . . . To be sure, it is not *Ratio*, the star-eyed goddess of the lawyers, who gives advice to the Prince; however, *Ratio* is not absent from the image. In the circle above the emperor's head we recognize the Holy Spirit descending from heaven in the shape of the dove, the symbol also of Divine Wisdom and Reason. . . . In this scene of judgment Henry II clearly functions as mediator between divine Reason and human Law. But, as behooves an Ottonian Prince, the emperor's mediatorship is expressed "liturgically," that is, by the *epiklesis* of the Spirit. The picture's language is theological, and not jurisprudential: the emperor is mediator and executor of the divine will through the power of the Holy Spirit, and not through the secular spirit of legal science. (*ibid.*, p. 115)

These two different but related examples are very important for future development, and for Dante's personal viewpoint. As a matter of fact, while the first was emphasized by Frederick II and his *logothetes*, Pier delle Vigne: "The Emperor was enthroned in serene detachment above the multitude, while like *an officiating priest* Piero della Vigna stood by his side and communicated to the audience the oracle of the imperial Godhead while the people bowed the knee before his majesty" (my italics);[69] the second appears closer to the ideals of Dante, who seems to hold to a less drastic and, in a way, less pre-Renaissance attitude, in spite of the evident relationship between the ideals and the programme of Frederick II and Dante.

But what is important now is the inference from the fact that Dante, to quote Gilson, "was able to raise up a universal Monarch vis-à-vis the universal Pope only by imagining this Monarch himself as a kind of Pope";[70] therefore the counsellors of the Emperor, the *litterati* as the jurists called themselves, became the counterparts of the cardinals, and Justice, since her colour is white (*Mon.* I, xi, 4: ". . . quemadmodum *albedo* in suo abstracto considerata"), became, because of the role of purification played by the Seven Virtues, a counterpart of baptism ("Quantum ergo ad habitum, iustitia contrarietatem habet quandoque in velle; nam ubi voluntas ab omni cupiditate sincera non est, etsi adsit iustitia, non tamen omnino inest *in fulgore sue puritatis*" *Ibid.* I, xi, 6; my italics).

This must be taken into account in order to understand how and why Dante could re-instate *humanitas* as opposed to *christianitas* (considered historically), not through a sacramental act, but because of man's powers, that is to say, by natural reason and by intellectual virtues. This also accounts for Dante's recovery of the Graeco-Roman tradition, that is, his concern with the whole of mankind[71] and the salvation of the righteous pagans such as Trajan the Emperor and Rhipeus the Trojan, although this salvation was only possible through Predestination and through the intervention of God's grace. Cato (*pro*

[69]E. Kantorowicz, *Frederick the Second, 1194–1250*, trans. E. O. Lorimer (New York, 1957), 513.

[70]Gilson, *Dante the Philosopher*, 179.

[71]As a typical example, *pro totalitate*, let us refer to the *Saladino*, and quote from an outstanding and highly stimulating article of Américo Castro, "Présence du Sultan Saladin dans les littératures romaines," in *Diogène*, VIII (1954), p. 9: "Dante ne loue pas la libéralité comme le ferait un écrivain quémandeur avide de faciles bénéfices, non, il pense à la qualité royale et illustre de ces grands seigneurs dont les Médicis allaient plus tard continuer la lignée. Saladin sera le seul musulman exempté de peines éternelles, Dante le plaçant dans les limbes, au milieu des héros de l'antiquité: 'e solo in parte vidi il Saladino' (*Inf.* IV, 129)."

tempore) and Virgil are not saved, nor do they "put on" the theological virtues, therefore they are not admitted beyond Purgatory and the earthly Paradise. But Virgil, by prophetic inspiration, could help Statius obtain salvation.

Here I emphasize the verses in which Virgil's role is once again clearly interrelated with the word *battesmo*. In the *Purgatorio* (XXII, 55), Virgil, here very allusively called "cantor de' bucolici carmi," asks Statius:

> Or quando tu cantasti le crude armi
> de la doppia tristizia di Iocasta—
> disse il cantor de' bucolici carmi—,

> per quello che Cliò teco lì tasta,
> non par che ti facesse ancor fedele
> la fede, sanza qual ben far non basta.

Statius answers:

> ". . . Tu prima m'inviasti
> verso Parnaso a ber ne le sue grotte,
> e prima appresso Dio m'alluminasti.

> Facesti come quei che va di notte,
> che porta il lume dietro e sé non giova,
> ma dopo sé fa le persone dotte,

> quando dicesti: 'Secol si rinnova;
> torna giustizia e primo tempo umano,
> e progenie scende da ciel nova!'

> Per te poeta fui, per te cristiano:

> · · · · · · · · · · · ·

> E pria ch'io conducessi i Greci a' fiumi
> di Tebe poetando, ebb'io battesmo."

There is a new element here, a relationship between Parnassus and Statius' drinking and earthly Paradise and Dante's drinking at the twin streams of Lethe and Eunoë; the prophetic and soteriological value of the messianic Eclogue of Virgil; the reference to the benefit granted by Virgil to those who followed him, but above all the striking relationship, expressed twice, between poetry (*poeta-poetando*) and Christianity (*cristiano-battesmo*).

It should not be forgotten that upon Dante's arrival in the earthly Paradise, it is by no mere coincidence that voices, in a very allusive

manner, pronounce "Adam," as a greeting to Dante, and that moreover the poet, immediately after, reminds us of the myth of the
golden age sung by the ancient poets, and of the innocence of the
root of all man's seed:

> Quelli ch'anticamente poetaro
> l'età dell'oro e suo stato felice,
> forse in Parnaso esto loco sognaro.
>
> Qui fu innocente l'umana radice;
> qui primavera sempre ed ogni frutto;
> nettare è questo di che ciascun dice
>
> (*Purg.* XXVIII, 139–144).

These verses and the name of Adam now appear more clearly defined
in a union of the whole *humanitas-christianitas* summed up in the
Christian poet himself.

But even though Dante reached the intermediate end—Beatrice and
the Earthly Paradise—through his own endeavours, nevertheless, to
be carried through the heavens and to be granted the ultimate end,
he needed the mercy of God. All the intermediary steps guide us to a
full understanding of the significance of the gradual centrifugal dilatation of Canto VI in each of the three canticles which deal with
Florence (*Inf.* VI.), Italy (*Purg.* VI), and the Empire (*Par.* VI);
moreover, Justinian was chosen instead of Constantine to pronounce
the solemn encomium of the Empire, since the latter was guilty not
only of conferring, through the Donation, temporal power to the Pope,
thus permitting, as Pietrobono has stressed, Adam's new sin, but also,
by transferring the Empire to Greece, "contra'l corso del cielo," of
causing another no less sinful and disruptive discord in the harmony
of the Universe.

This same dilatation, or expansion, indicates that man is simultaneously a member of the three communities—city, country, and
Empire—and it also reveals the polymorphic goal of Dante's mission,
from the salvation of mankind realized for the whole of humanity in
the salvation of one man, to the salvation of the city, the country,
the Empire, and the Church—combined in the *corpus Christi, figura-
liter*—due to perfectibility shown and described by the poet, truly the
scriba Dei, chosen *gratia Dei*, as the mediator between spiritual and
material power, between heaven and earth.

This union of the past, the present, and the future, represented by the whole history of mankind comprehending earth and heaven, macrocosmic-microcosmic harmony, beginning and end, is a gigantic task which Dante was the first to undertake.

In the very first line of the *Divina Commedia*, "Nel mezzo del cammin di nostra vita," there appears, as we know, both the singular-plural presence of the poet and of mankind, and the idea of the poet's motion, represented by the word *cammin* and that of mankind implicit in *nostra vita*. There is circular symmetry and, simultaneously, an analogical thesis—antithesis with the very last line of the sacred poem: "l'Amor che muove il sole e l'altre stelle." These lines can be opposed to each other in the following manner: "selva oscura → sole"; "anabasis of the poet-mankind → katabasis of the poet-mankind within the motion of the Universe." This motion of the poet-mankind, imposed by the *vacatio Imperii* and therefore by *Justitiae* (*Mon.* II, ix, 1–2: "Namque ubicumque humanum iudicium deficit, vel ignorantie tenebris involutum vel propter presidium iudicis non habere, ne iustitia derelicta remaneat, *recurrendum est ad Illum* qui tantum eam dilexit ut, quod ipsa exigebat, de proprio sanguine ipse morienda supplevit; unde psalmus: 'Justus Dominus et iustitiam dilexit." my italics), will lead him to the heavenly Jerusalem, "quod interpretatur Visio pacis," as has been thoroughly discussed in the exegetical lore, "per vedere," before his *militia litterata* begins with a prophetic (*altro vello*) voice (*altra voce*). But first he must have, although it is only suggested, the same consecration that Virgil, perhaps in an antitypical way, has granted him in the *Purgatorio* (XXVII, 142), with the much discussed line: "per ch'io te sovra te corono e mitrio." But if the coronation by Virgil was only para-sacramental, the threefold blessing of St. Peter acquires a double meaning in relation to the font when we bear in mind that ever since the earliest days of the Church the baptismal unction was understood in the sense which St. Peter gave it when addressing the converts (I Peter, 2:9): "Ye are a chosen generation, a royal priesthood." If to this is added that "Durandus mentions for the province of Narbonne the custom of applying a red trimming *in modum coronae* to the cap of the chrisom, the white baptismal robe, which may hardly have differed from the red-trimmed *coiffe*, the linen cap for the protection of the holy oil, with which the head of the baptized was covered *quasi quadam mitra*,"[72] we shall almost have

[72]Kantorowicz, *The King's Two Bodies*, 490.

established the identification of St. Peter Damian's hat not with the biretta but with a mitre which we considered earlier. This now, related to the word *poeta*, designates Dante's "imperium Pagina sacra," provided, in order to complete John of Salisbury's thought, "Cum cunctas artes, cum dogmata cuncta penitus/noverit"; in other words, *poema sacro*, the *Divina Commedia*, which stands for theological poetry.[73]

The theological poetry of the *Divina Commedia* must be considered, then, as a further step from the earlier definition of *poeta rectitudinis*, which we find in the *De Vulgari Eloquentia* (II, ii, 8–9).

As a matter of fact, only this new theological poetry will enable the poet to come to an identification of his katabasis and mission.

Upon the attainment and contemplation of God and the restoration of tradition and after entry into the harmonious motion of the Universe together with the disparate facets of Creation which are summed up in God, when, from the moment *desiderium Dantis* and the twofold *velle* (*voluntas Dantis* and *voluntas Dei*) achieve through Providence a perfect coincidence, the katabasis, with all its fateful and providential implications, *consummata erit*[74]–the katabasis, whose twofold possibility derives from the fact that the poet is at the same time both the protagonist (the mission begins in the year 1300, when Dante still lived in Florence) and the author, and therefore the Poem, a fact which implies an *a quo* and a *sub specie aeternitatis*, because the *Commedia* itself is both *in* and *out* of time, which corresponds to the "multiple end" stated in the letter to Can Grande (*Ep.* XIII, 39): "Finis totius et partis esse posset et multiplex, scilicet *propinquus* et *remotus*. . . ."

[73]"Quella di 'poema sacro' non è una mera immagine. Sacrale nell'accezione teologica, dualistica, intellettuale (anche se mira, lo dice l'epistola, sia qui all'azione, con alla speculazione) sono predicati che vanno insieme; e dànno ragione alla particolare formulazione che assume il personaggio che dice 'io' presso un genio dell'estate del Medioevo." (Contini, *Supra* n. 35, 46).

[74]As a complementary suggestion here, since it is again to baptism and the *nominum interpretationem*, let me repeat what I pointed out elsewhere (see my "Dante 'scriba Dei'," and particularly 414–422, "quod interpretatur Dantis": equazione tipologica Natàn-Dante), that the name of Dante is the Latin *interpretatio* of the name of the prophet Nathan, et *per consequens*, of the prophet's mission.

The Twins of Latona

AND OTHER SYMMETRICAL
SYMBOLS FOR JUSTICE IN DANTE

ERICH VON RICHTHOFEN

DANTE, WHO WAS born under the constellation of Gemini, has a marked tendency to express himself in similes designating pairs or couples. To this group of images belongs that of Latona's children, and also other symmetrical symbols reflecting some fundamental aspects of Dante's complex conception of justice.[1]

Let me begin with a brief comment on the poet's characteristic technique of contrasting geometrically two extreme poles. This is done in order to harmonize them, for instance papal and imperial power, or to oppose them as irreconcilable expressions of good and evil, as that of *veltro* and *lupa*, the hound and the she-wolf. Most of these images reveal a multiplicity of aspects. Other examples are the long discussed, but still controversial *tra Feltro e Feltro* in *Inferno* I, 105, as well as *tra Saturno e Marte* in the *Sonetto* XXVIII, 3, referring to the *temprata stella* in *Paradiso* XVIII, 68. The latter represents Jupiter ruling that part of heaven where dwell the souls of the just, between the supposedly frigid planet, Saturn, and the warm planet, Mars. A similar antithesis or parallel is that between Mars, the god of antiquity, and Saint John the Baptist, in *tra Marte e 'l Batista*

---

[1]This brief analysis will be linked to studies which I have published earlier. Its main purpose, however, is to present additional considerations for the first time. Since to a large extent they have developed independently from A. Gilbert, *Dante's Conception of Justice* (1925), and G. Ursini, *La Giustizia nel Poema di Dante* (1955), it is hoped that they will shed some more light upon the subject treated in these basic informative works.

(*Par.* XVI, 47), symbolizing the evil pagan spirit of war and confusion opposed to genuine love among Christians. Apollo and Diana are mentioned as a pair, *ambedue li figli di Latona* (*Paradiso* XXIX, 1), and are also called *li due occhi del cielo.* In *Purgatorio* XX, 132, this image refers to Apollo's identification with the sun and Diana's with the moon; in *De Monarchia* I, 11, it is a symbol contrasting papal and imperial power. Then there are the two luminous figures of Saint Peter and Saint James in *Paradiso* XXIV–XXV; they were emissaries of Christ and to their memory were erected the sanctuaries of Rome and Santiago de Compostela, respectively, the main destinations of pilgrimages during the Middle Ages.[2] Among the more briefly mentioned pairs we find Charlemagne and Roland; Guillaume d'Orange and Rainouart; Godfrey of Bouillon and Robert Guiscard. They all distinguished themselves in the struggles against the enemies of Christianity,[3] and significantly, are rewarded in Paradise (*Par.* XVIII, 43–48).

Most of these images give evidence of Dante's familiarity with the mythology of the ancient Greek and Latin poetry as well as with the legends of the mediaeval epic. They are usually linked to the author's concept of justice, of which they constitute an important aspect. This is truly the case with the frequent reference made to the twins of Latona. The Greek titaness Leto, called Latona by Virgil and Ovid, was the daughter of Coeus and Phoebe. She was chiefly known as the mother of Apollo, the god of the sun, and Artemis the huntress, with whom the Italian goddess Diana had anciently been identified. Before their birth, Hera, called Juno by the Romans, was jealous of Zeus/ Jupiter's love for Latona and therefore persecuted the latter who finally wandered to Delos, a floating island, which now was fixed by Jupiter to the bottom of the sea with adamantine chains. Dante compares the shaking of Mount Purgatory to the tossing of Delos before Latona gave birth to the twins:

> Certo non si scotea sì forte Delo,
> pria che Latona in lei facesse 'l nido
> a parturir li due occhi del cielo.
>
> (*Purg.* XX, 130–132)

---

[2] See my "Notas sobre Temas épico-medievales," in *Boletín de Filología*, XI, 1959 (publ. 1960), 353 ff. Cf. also *Bol. Fil.*, XII (1960, publ. 1961), 44, n. 220.

[3] Already earlier Charlemagne had come to the help of the Church in Lombardy: "E quando il dente longobardo morse / la Santa Chiesa, sotto le sue ali / Carlo Magno, vincendo, la soccorse" (*Par.* VI, 94–96).

The latter, of course, are Apollo and Diana, also called Delius and Delia from their birthplace. The mountain trembles when justice is finally done to a soul which, after accomplishing atonement, is ascending from Purgatory to Paradise (*Purg.* XXI, 37 ff.).

The most favourable condition under which justice is possible seems indicated in the *De Monarchia* as well as in the *Paradiso*. It is at the times of the equinox that both Latona's children, identified with the sun and the moon, achieve balance on opposite sides of the horizon. They stand for the Pontiff and the Emperor in a reference to them in one of Dante's epistles (VI, 8). This is explained in the *Paradiso*:

> Quando ambedue li figli di Latona,
>   coperti del Montone e della Libra,
>   fanno dell'orizzonte insieme zona.   (XXIX, 1–3)

The sun stands here under the sign of the Ram, and the moon under that of the Scales, the latter being also regarded as a symbol of justice. The pertinent text in the *De Monarchia* is: "Ubi ergo minimum de contrario iustitie admiscetur et quantum ad habitum et quantum ad operationem, ibi iustitia potissima est; . . . est enim tunc Phebe [under which name the moon is equally known] similis, fratrem diametraliter intuenti de purpureo matutine serenitatis" (I, 11). Under this—rather infrequent—condition it is most possible for true human justice to be achieved. Dante's concept of human justice may be summed up by this simile, which also suggests the image of the balance of justice. However, as the moon receives the light from the sun, so the emperor is dependent on the pontiff in some ways, since earthly wisdom remains subordinate to the eternal. Whether this concept is based on Dante's idea of the Carolingian empire, on the Justinian order, or perhaps on Averroes, is not our immediate concern.

Let us consider another aspect of the same simile. Dante himself had begun his wanderings through the realms of the beyond, which made him worthy of grace and acquainted him with the divine justice, under precisely the sign of the sun and the moon in its full round at the time of the Easter equinox. This he explained retrospectively to Forese Donati (*Purg.* XXIII, 118–121):

> Di quella vita mi volse costui
>   che mi va innanzi, l'altrier, quando tonda
>   vi si mostrò la suora di colui;
> e 'l sol mostrai.   (i.e. Virgil)

In the *Commedia*, which foreshadows the world beyond the last judgment, the term *giustizia* is used as often as thirty-six times, and in his Latin works *iustitia* occurs forty-five times. It designates either the ability to judge justly, or the divine justice. God himself is called "la giustizia sempiterna" in *Paradiso* XIX, 58; and the spirits conspicuous for justice manifest themselves in lights forming the letters of the Latin sentence "DILIGITE IUSTITIAM . . . QUI IUDICATIS TERRAM" in *Paradiso* XVIII, 91 and 93. The whole sentence, which copies the beginning of the *Liber Sapientiae* is the only one of the *Commedia* written exclusively in capital letters, apart from the inscription at the entrance to Hell in *Inferno* III, 1–9, among which we find also: "GIUSTIZIA MOSSE IL MIO ALTO FATTORE." *Iustitia* is furthermore the topic of several chapters in Dante's *De Monarchia*. It is in this treatise that the author uses the simile of Phoebe and Phoebus (for the moon and the sun) which we have discussed.

Divine justice was the main act witnessed by the wanderer through the realms of the beyond, while civic justice had become a matter of greatest concern for the exiled citizen of Florence. "Iustitia . . . revirescet," we read in *Epistola* V on the divine mission of the emperor Henry VII; and "Iustitia potissima est solum sub Monarcha," "quemadmodum cupiditas habitualem iustitiam . . . obnubilat,"[4] are among the numerous similar statements in *De Monarchia* I, 11. Substantially, they reflect Aristotelian thought as transmitted by the Scholastics, Saint Thomas Aquinas in particular. As Dante has in mind the Christian emperor—such as Charlemagne—who receives his light from the Church, his concept of the monarch implies divine assistance in the activities of his wordly power, among which the foremost is justice.

In the *Commedia*, after the Cacciaguida cantos in which mention is made also of Charlemagne and Roland (*Par.* XVIII, 43), Dante ascends to the heaven of the planet Jupiter placed "tra 'l padre e 'l figlio," according to *Paradiso* XXII, 147. It is here that the spirits are manifested in lights, transforming the final M of the last word first into the pattern of a lily and then into that of an eagle. The latter is more than the symbol of an earthly empire alone; its function is extended as is that of Beatrice in the *Commedia* who is representative of more than mere feminine virtues. This appears to be in accordance also with the

---

[4]Cf. also "Cum . . . cupiditas ipsa sola sit . . . iustitiae praepeditiva" (*De Mon.* I, 13).

inner development of the *comedìa,* as the work was initially called by Dante (*Inf.* XVI, 128; XXI, 2), into a "poema sacro," as it is referred to at a later stage (*Par.* XXIII, 62; XXV, 1). It is interesting that the expression *sacri poëmatis* had once been applied to Virgil by Macrobius (*Saturnalia* I, 24). In *Purgatorio* IX, 70–72, we read:

> Lettor, tu vedi ben com'io innalzo
> la mia matera, e però con più arte
> non ti meravigliar s'io la rincalzo.

The imperial eagle states that divine justice can differ from what is understood as justice on earth. Similarly (*Par.* IV, 67–69), Beatrice had explained to Dante:

> Parere ingiusta la nostra giustizia
> nelli occhi de' mortali, è argomento
> di fede e non d'eretica nequizia.

To this corresponds the *Trasumanar significar per verba / non si porìa . . .* of *Paradiso* I, 70–71.

Divine justice is thus often referred to as being not fully comprehensible and therefore ineffable, or it is circumscribed by the introduction of seemingly obscure symbols taken preferably from biblical, liturgical, and related usage.[5] Corresponding analogies are also established in similes designating human justice, in which reference to ancient myth and oracles seems to prevail, though divine assistance is still implied. This technique of poetic expression becomes evident in the contrasting images of Mars and the Baptist, standing for distructive woe and for peaceful Christian weal, respectively, as well as in those of the twins of Latona—Apollo and Diana—in the *De Monarchia* and the *Commedia*. If the twins are in perfect harmony (thus representing the appropriate moment for justice on earth), the former remain in extreme disharmony.

Key images are often extended in the *Commedia* by later retrospective references, or they are introduced by a briefer mention in an early passage in order to prepare for their subsequent appearance in full light and wider context. Frequently they are also linked to other similes illustrating either parallel concepts or their antonyms, thus

---

[5]One possible exception: when Dante composed the last verse of the *Commedia,* "L'amor che move il sole e l'altre stelle" (*Par.* XXXIII, 145), he may have recalled Boethius' "amor, / quo caeeum regitur" in *De Consolatione Philosophiae,* VIII, quoted in *De Mon.* I, 9.

establishing an interrelation between a larger group of ideas. At times synonymous similes with a more limited meaning, as well as terms used in an extended or more specific connotation, are juxtaposed. Thus, Apollo is referred to as "delfica deità" in *Paradiso* I, 22, because of his famous oracle at Delphi where his main temple stood. The name Diana, which usually refers to "la figlia di Latona" (*Par.* X, 67; XXII, 139), was also applied to a river supposed to exist underneath the city of Siena. This legendary stream was never found, but the Sienese in Dante's time still nourished "la speranza . . . a trovar la Diana" (*Purg.* XIII, 153). The alleged subterranean river owed this name to a belief that a statue of the goddess had once stood on the market place of Siena.

Another legendary temple and statue which are repeatedly mentioned in the *Commedia* are those of the god of war, Mars. Dante, referring to the citizens of Florence says:

> Molti han giustizia in cuore, e tardi scocca
> per non venir sanza consiglio all'arco;
> ma il popol tuo l'ha in sommo della bocca.
>
> (*Purg.* VI, 130–132)

meaning thereby that many who bear the concept of justice in their heart only speak of it, instead of performing it. Florence is the city which turned from its first patron (Mars) and chose the Baptist, though the evil spirit still remained visible on the bank of the Arno, where the statue of Mars was placed after the city's destruction. In the chronicles, this had been attributed to the king of the Huns, Attila, who was confused with Totila:

> I' fui de la città che nel Batista
> mutò il primo padrone; ond' è per questo
>
> Sempre con l'arte sua la farà trista;
> e se non fosse che 'n sul passo d'Arno
> rimane ancor di lui alcuna vista,
>
> Que' cittadin che poi la rifondarno
> sovra 'l cener che d'Attila rimase,
> avrebber fatto lavorare indarno   (*Inf.* XIII, 143–150)

Cacciaguida's expression "tra Marte e 'l Batista", refers to the equestrian statue which used to stand where the Ponte Vecchio was built, and to the Battistero di San Giovanni which, itself, is a converted temple of Mars. When the church was dedicated in the fourth century, the statue of the pagan deity may have been removed to the Arno. (However, *Mars* could well be a corruption of *Marcus*, thus referring to an equestrian statue of Marcus Aurelius, later mistaken for that of the god of war.)[6] In Totila's time the image fell into the river; in the Carolingean era it was placed on a pillar near the Arno, and during the flood of 1333 it disappeared in the water. Boccaccio states that it was recovered later in a weather-beaten condition. This would correspond to what was already pointed out by Dante, who referred to it as "pietra scema"

> Ma convenìesi a quella pietra scema
> che guarda 'l ponte che Firenze fesse
> vittima nella sua pace postrema.
>
> (*Par.* XVI, 145–147)

The simile "between Mars and the Baptist" refers to the location of Florence—and consequently its way of life—between evil and good, as long as justice is not established in fulfilment of the initial prophecy of the *veltro* which, in the striking simile of *Inferno* I, 101, was contrasted with the allegory of the *lupa*, an incarnation of human avidity still ruling Italy in Dante's era.

The enigmatic *veltro* oracle, too, is an expression of the concept of justice in Dante. Most attempts to identify it have so far pointed to an emperor, either of human or divine origin, or, as I have suggested in the past, it may embody the figure of a helper who became instrumental in the re-establishment and the defence of a Christian empire, such as that of Charlemagne. This approach to the *Commedia* is determined by an effort not only to regard Dante as an exponent of Scholastic theology and as the *sommo poeta* of the mediaeval period in Italy, but to see him particularly in his relation to the epic poetry of the western world, classical as well as mediaeval,[7] including the structural devices, symbols, similes, and the style which these works have

---

[6]Cf. E. Von Richthofen, *Veltro und Diana—Dantes mittelalterliche und antike Gleichnisse* (Tübingen, 1956), 5.

[7]According to legendary tradition, the Merovingian king, Clovis I, who is Floovant in the French epic and Fioravante in Italian adaptations, was born with a sign on his shoulder: "nacque. . . . con una croce di sangue tra pelle e pelle" (*Reali di Francia*), which was taken for an indication that he would be king of what was later called France (*Storia di Fioravante*). Cf. *Veltro und Diana*, 21 f. (Old French *feltrez* has been related to the skin of children). In a late English prose adaptation of the mediaeval legend *Ponthus and Sidone*, Brodas, the son of the

in common. In a book published in 1956[8] I showed that the only work in which a *veltro* had a similar function as that indicated by Dante was the *Song of Roland*, composed two centuries before the *Commedia*. A possible relation between the two corresponding allegories had already been supposed by other critics, but this problem was not studied in the light of the idea of justice linked also to the ancient myth of Diana, who is often represented with her hunting dog. Diana's task was not unlike that of Opis, sent out by Diana's mother Latona in Virgil's Camilla episode. Dante refers to it immediately after formulating the *veltro* prophecy in *Inferno* I, 101–111:

> . . . infin che 'l Veltro
> verrà, che la farà morir con doglia.
>
> · · · · · · · · · · · · ·
>
> Di quella umile Italia fia salute
> per cui morì la vergine Cammilla,
> Eurialo e Turno e Niso di ferute.
>
> Questi la caccerà per ogni villa,
> fin che l'avrà rimessa nello 'nferno,
> là onde invidia prima dipartilla.

Cupidity is the worst enemy of justice: "quod iustitiae maxime contrariatur cupiditas" (*De Mon.* I, 11). However, when cupidity is removed altogether, nothing remains inimical to justice: "Remota cupiditate omnino, nihil iustitiae restat adversum" (*De Mon.* I, 11). In *De Consolatione Philosophiae* IV of Boethius, one of Dante's favourite Latin poets, he had found the comparison of *avaritia* with a wolf: "Avaritia fervet alienarum opum violentus ereptor: lupus similem diceris." The parallelism of the mediaeval *veltro* prophecy and the ancient Camilla episode appears evident; the latter serves to explain the former, which cannot be evaluated independently from the other.

The purpose of the greyhound's mission for Dante, like that of Opis for Virgil (*Æneid*, XI, 532 ff.; 588 ff.), was to re-establish right in fulfilment of divine will. It was also that of the *veltres* in the *Song of Roland*—a symbol for Thierry of Ripuaria,[9] who was doing for the

---

sultan of Babylon and lord of Galicia in Spain, dreams that he has been transformed into a wolf and is vanquished by a hound: "I dremed this night that I become a grete, black wolfe, and that sett upon me a grete, whyte grehounde and a brachete, and the grehounde sleve me" (ed. F. J. Mather Jr., in *PMLA*, XII (1897), 113).

[8]*Veltro and Diana*, see note 6.

[9]See *Veltro und Diana*, 31 f. In Dante's Italy, Can Grande della Scala was

empire he was serving precisely what was carried out by Latona's
helper in Virgil and what is expected of the hound for Italy in Dante:
the re-establishment of justice and order. In the *Song of Roland*[10]
the latter is achieved by a duel which provokes and obtains divine
justice. Dante dedicates an extensive passage to this custom in the
De Monarchia II, 9, with reference to St. Matthew 28:20.

It is not possible here to go into the numerous details and the variety
of aspects which these comparisons reveal. I may however turn to
another work of mediaeval literature, Brunetto Latini's *Tesoretto*,
which was well known to Dante and which refers directly to Roncevaux, the site of the injustice done to Roland and avenged by
Thierry. After passages concerning the struggle between the Ghibel-
lines and the Guelfs in Florence, the author relates that he lost his
path near Roncevaux, entered a forest, and met some animals before
having his own vision of Nature, Virtue, and her daughters Wisdom,
Temperance, Strength, and Justice. He says:

> Certo lo cor mi parte
> di cotanto dolore,
> pensando 'l grande onore
> e la ricca potenza
> che suole aver Florenza
> quasi nel mondo tutto.
> Ond'io in tal corrotto
> pensando, a capo chino,
> perdei lo gran cammino,
> e tenno ala traversa
> d'una selva diversa.
>
> Ma tornando ala mente
> mi volsi e posi mente
> intorno ala montagna,
> E vidi turba magna
> di diversi animali,
> che non so ben dir quali,
> ma omini e mogliere,
> bestie, serpent' e fiere (v. 180–199).

---

appointed Imperial Vicar in Verona and Vicenza by Henry VII (Moroello Malaspina
appeared to be sent to Brescia in a similar function).

[10]Cf. my studies "La Justice dans l'épilogue de la Chanson de Roland et du
Poème du Cid," in *Cahiers de civilisation médiévale*, III (1960), 76 ff.; and "Notas
sobre Temas épico-medievales," in *Boletín de Filología*, XI, 1959 (publ. 1960),
chapter on "Justicia: El Mito de las dos Espadas del Cid," 346 ff.

He finds himself later in a desert, of which the introductory verses of the *Commedia* seem to remind us:

> E non fui guari andato,
> ch'i' fui nella deserta
> dov'io non trovai certa
> nè strada nè sentero.
> Deh, che paese fero
> trovai in quella parte!
> Chè, quanto più mirava,
> più mi parea salvagio.
>
> Ma ricontar non oso
> ciò ch'io trovai e vidi (v. 1188–1197; 1224–1225)

This would indicate that Dante's familiarity with the myth of Roncevaux came not only from the *Song of Roland*, of which important manuscripts have been preserved in Venice, but also from the *Tesoretto*.

If the theoretical discussions of the idea of justice, particularly in the *De Monarchia*, show that the works of the Scholastics, including Canon Law, lie at the basis of his conception, the poetic similes used by Dante are preferably taken from ancient mythology and mediaeval epics. This harmonizing or contrasting technique, which combined and integrated the plasticity of the Virgilian imagery, reshaped and extended by Dante, was certainly a unique achievement at this period of the late Middle Ages, which had also produced such metrical innovations as the endecasyllabic verse of the sonnet and the *terza rima*. The new method and techniques became models for subsequent generations of poets, from Petrarch to Michelangelo in Italy, and as late as Milton in England.[11]

Besides the biblical, hagiographic, or liturgical elements assimilated in the *Commedia*, as well as Aristotelianism or mediaeval Platonism transmitted by the Scholastics, Dante also revived or transformed aspects of the works of the Roman authors, Virgil, Statius, Lucan,

---

[11]Even in our own century, an author like Gerhart Hauptmann has ventured to compose in *terza rima* a dantesque vision of the beyond in his *Der grosse Traum* (cf. my articles "Gerhart Hauptmann und Dante," in *Archiv f. d. Stud. d. Neueren Sprachen*, vol. 187, 1950, 76 ff.; and "Italienische und mögliche spanische Einflüsse in Gerhart Hauptmanns Traumdichtungen," in *Studia Philologica*, Homenaje a Dámaso Alonso, vol. III (1963), 161 ff.

Ovid, Boethius, etc., the myths of the sphinx, the Lethe, of Themis,[12] Camilla, Diana, Apollo, Odysseus, Castor and Pollux, and others. Similarly, the mediaeval French and Italian epic legends were used by him as sources of inspiration. The influence of *Roland* and of the *Tesoretto* gives evidence of this, as well as the mention made of Lancelot, Tristan, Hugo Capet, Roland, Guillaume d'Orange and Arnaut Daniel, among many others. To a higher degree than any other mediaeval author, Dante linked the traditions of theology and of literature. Here the barriers fell, so that both could be assimilated and developed further. A typically poetic combination of the Christian with the mythological is the invocation of the "somme Giove . . . per noi crucifisso" in *Purgatorio* VI, 118–119. In this fusion, or contrasting, of concepts taken from either sphere—affecting the whole range of the references given to his symbols—Dante went far beyond the technique of other epic authors, whether mediaeval Latin or Romance. Poetry, under his inspiration, took a most significant step forward, not only within the evolution of the mediaeval writings, but also in preparation for a new period, the path which was to be followed by the Muses of the Renaissance.

[12]The Greek prophetess and representative of firmly established law and justice is referred to in Ovid, *Met.* I, 379–380, and Dante, *Purg.* XXXIII, 37–51.